Georg Heym

A Reluctant Rebel

Georg Heym
Jugendbildnis, die einzige erhal=
tene Photographie, im Besitze des
Kurt Wolff=Verlags, München

Georg Heym

A Reluctant Rebel

by

Egbert Krispyn

Gainesville

UNIVERSITY OF FLORIDA PRESS

1968

A University of Florida Press Book

Library of Congress
Catalog Card No. 68-28871

PRINTED AND BOUND FOR THE PUBLISHER BY
STORTER PRINTING COMPANY, INCORPORATED
GAINESVILLE, FLORIDA
AND
DOBBS BROTHERS LIBRARY BINDING COMPANY, INCORPORATED
HIALEAH, FLORIDA

Contents

Introduction

EXPRESSIONIST LITERATURE was the swan song of the German Empire. Between 1910 and 1914 the movement developed its essential character as a reaction against the mental atmosphere of the Empire under Wilhelm II. The momentum gathered in these years carried expressionism through the following period of war and revolution. However, these upheavals stimulated the development of imitative and propagandistic elements in the movement, whose nature was thereby significantly changed. The qualitative climax of pure expressionism occurred before World War I, although quantitatively the movement's literary output reached its peak later. With the Weimar Republic, new literary currents took over. Expressionism, however, had left a very vivid memory, and for about a decade after it had run its course, numerous attempts were made to analyze and describe it.

Then, for many years, expressionism was hushed up and all but forgotten. But when, after World War II, the Germans probed their literary past to find a basis for a fresh start, they did not hit firm ground until they had gone back in time to the turbulent decade 1910-20. With very few exceptions the expressionists were dead. Two wars, persecution, and exile had taken a heavy toll among them. But expressionism, the creation of their youth, proved to be a solid foundation for the literature which, through such writers as Günter Grass, Heinrich Böll, Günter Eich, Martin Wal-

1

ser, Uwe Johnson, Ilse Aichinger, Ingeborg Bachmann, Max Frisch, Friedrich Dürrenmatt, and others, has gained worldwide repute.

Postwar literary scholarship has duly acknowledged the importance of expressionism. The last fifteen years have produced a plethora of dissertations, essays, monographs, and collected editions in this field.* These documents reveal that the relative merits of some prominent expressionists are now judged differently than during the time of the movement and the years immediately following it.

Georg Heym is one of those whose artistic reputation has been affected by this process of reevaluation. Until the advent of the Third Reich, when the Nazis outlawed the whole of expressionism as "decadent" and interrupted the public discussion on this subject for almost fifteen years, Heym was ranked as a notable but not supremely important exponent of the movement.

Franz Werfel, on the other hand, was generally regarded as the most prominent lyric poet of the generation, in spite of such dissenting voices as that of Ferdinand Josef Schneider, who accused him of "speculative sentimentality."[1] Among the dramatists "under the spell of expressionism,"† Georg Kaiser occupied a position of comparable preeminence, and Carl Sternheim was also frequently seen as a more important figure than Heym.

Looking back on expressionism from a post-World-War-II standpoint, the earlier judgments have lost their validity. Werfel's earlier work is completely overshadowed by his subsequent achievements, and Kaiser's relations with expressionism are, in recent studies, either inadequately dealt with,[2] regarded as only a relatively minor passing phase,[3] or virtually denied.[4] Carl Sternheim's importance is the subject of controversy,[5] while Georg Heym's poetry now appears to be one of the most valuable manifestations of the expressionist movement in any literary genre.

This development is, as far as lyric poetry is concerned, to some extent reflected in the composition of the various anthologies— only to some extent, since the recent ones serve a literary-*historical* interest and therefore try to reflect the state of the expressionist

*Richard Brinkmann, *Expressionismus. Forschungs-Probleme 1952-1960* (Stuttgart, 1961), lists almost 300 titles for the eight years between 1952 and 1960 alone, not counting 51 dissertations during the period 1952-58.

†"Im Banne des Expressionismus." This expression was coined by Albert Soergel as the subtitle for his massive survey of the movement *Dichtung und Dichter der Zeit. Neue Folge. Im Banne des Expressionismus* (Leipzig, 1925).

era itself. Thus the publisher of the collection *Lyrik des expression-istischen Jahrzehnts* states on the dust cover: "The selection aims at giving a record of that era and representing a great artistic movement, which was of German origin and found international recognition. Forgotten names and ones which are still famous today, poems of great originality, interesting experiments and works of perfection are here collected."[6] In spite of this intention, the editor has not been able to ignore the trend toward reevaluation completely. This is demonstrated by the fact that Heym is represented by twelve poems, and Werfel by only ten. In the more scholarly anthology prepared by Clemens Heselhaus, six poems by each have been included.[7] The importance of these figures as an indication of a changed scale of values becomes clear from a comparison with Kurt Pinthus' famous anthology *Menschheitsdäm-merung* of 1920,[8] which contains thirteen works by Heym and more than twice as many by Werfel.

One may obtain further evidence of the reversal which has taken place in the appreciation of those still regarded as expressionists by comparing the measure of concern with these authors on the part of earlier and later literary historians. Of the near contemporary commentators, Albert Soergel in his comprehensive study devotes four pages to a discussion of Georg Heym, while he allots seventeen to Sternheim and no fewer than twenty to Werfel. In the recently reedited version of this work,[9] the respective figures are eight, sixteen, and fifteen. Although this does indicate a shift in emphasis in Heym's favor, it does not yet fully acknowledge the change in critical judgment since Soergel's day.

A more accurate indication of present-day views can be found in Richard Brinkmann's research report on expressionism for the period 1952-60. Brinkmann mentions three titles on Sternheim. Five studies on Werfel are included in the research report, but three of them are mainly concerned with his postexpressionistic writings.* Seven studies dealing exclusively with Heym are listed, and the important, extensive work by Kurt Mautz, which appeared in 1961, is not included among those. Neither are numerous articles in scholarly journals which, according to the reviewer, throw no new

---

*The same arithmetic could also be applied to Georg Kaiser, who received twenty-nine pages in Soergel's book and twenty in Hohoff's edition, and for whom Brinkmann lists only some six separate studies dealing wholly or in part with the work of the period concerned.

light on the subject matter, but which are nevertheless indicative of the authors' and the public's interest in Heym. A three-volume critical edition of all of Heym's writings has been published over a period of years,[10] and he has received due attention in most works dealing with expressionism as a whole. Moreover, daily newspapers in their feuilletons, and semipopular to popular periodicals such as *Der Monat, Das Schönste, Die Zeit,* and *Der Spiegel,* have on various occasions devoted considerable space to him.

In spite of all this activity, however, no serious attempt has yet been made to deal with the significance of Heym's life and work in the context of his time. The most recent and most ambitious work on him, Kurt Mautz' study *Mythologie und Gesellschaft im Expressionismus. Die Dichtung Georg Heyms,* concentrates, as the subtitle indicates, on the works. These are, of course, in themselves of far greater importance than the biographical details, but Mautz—who has a very keen eye for the inadequacies of preceding writers on the subject—falls prey to the great danger inherent in this strictly work-oriented approach. Apart from possible inaccuracies in Mautz' dating of the individual poems,[11] the main shortcoming of his study is that it presents Heym in a virtual literary vacuum. Although there is some historical perspective in Heym's relation to Jugendstil, Nietzsche, symbolism, and so forth, and in the mention of a few contemporary poets, there is not even a suggestion that Heym's work formed an integrated part of the literary production of his day. And yet this seems to be the most important aspect of the poet from the viewpoint of today. Valuable though many of his poems are in themselves, they gain their full significance only against the historical and literary background of the late Wilhelmian era.

Heym's biography at first sight appears almost disappointingly unexceptional, even trite. It is basically the same story as those of the majority of his contemporaries who have entered literary history. He could almost have stood as a model for Eduard Spranger's study on the psychology of the upper-middle-class youth of Wilhelmian Germany.[12] In spite, or rather because, of this, his case is valuable for an understanding of expressionism as a whole. In his own records of his rather uninteresting life, together with his work, we have the only sufficiently detailed and coherent body of information concerning the interrelationship of the Wilhelmian spirit, the individual personality, and the creative work.

Herewith the substance and structure of the present study are determined. Heym's biography is surveyed with specific regard to the development of his world view, and with reference to the general spirit prevailing in Wilhelmian bourgeois circles. His existential situation is then shown to have provided the basis of his writings—poetry, prose, and drama. For this purpose, only those works which he demonstrably intended for publication in their present form are taken into account. Especially in the case of a writer like Heym, who consciously worked on his writings until they conformed to his conception of the universe, it would be unjustifiable to draw conclusions from other manuscripts and plans found in his literary estate.

Finally an attempt is made to find the reason why now, fifty years after his death, Heym is more highly regarded than he was, in respect to other leading expressionists. Through the detailed investigation of those elements in his life and works which might be regarded as typical of his generation, this study, apart from presenting Heym and his work in the framework of his time, also attempts to supplement and substantiate my analysis of the expressionist movement as a whole.[13]

I

Sons and Fathers

GEORG THEODOR FRANZ ARTHUR HEYM was born on October 30, 1887, in the small Silesian town of Jelenia Góra (Hirschberg). His father Hermann Heym, who served the government as a legal functionary, came from a well-to-do Prussian landowning family. Georg's mother Jenny Taistrzit was also well situated. Her father and grandfather had possessed land and had held legal posts in Eastern Germany. Her great-grandfather had come from Hungary to Upper Silesia, where he probably owned an estate.

In 1889 Jenny Heym gave birth to her second and last child, a girl, who was named Gertrud. In 1894 Georg's father was transferred to Gniezno (Gnesen), where the boy, after Easter, 1896, attended the Gymnasium. In the summer of 1899 a further transfer of Hermann Heym took the family to Posen. There they remained for only a little more than a year, since in October, 1900, Hermann Heym was promoted to the position of military attorney at the Imperial military court in Berlin.[1]*

This city had undergone a startling metamorphosis since becoming the capital of the newly founded Reich. In the twenty-nine years that had elapsed since the political unification of Germany, the population of Berlin had grown almost four times as large, and the somewhat provincial Prussian town had turned into a

*Letters to and from Heym will be referred to by their numbers in Vol. III of *Dichtungen und Schriften*. Diary notes will be given by date only.

bustling metropolis. The same force which had swelled the number of Berliners to almost two million also made itself felt elsewhere in the country. During the period from 1871 to 1900, the total population of the Empire rose from 41 to 56 million. At the same time, the number of German cities of more than 100,000 inhabitants climbed from eight to thirty-three.[2]

The reason for this massive trek to the cities was the Industrial Revolution, which had reached Germany belatedly, in the wake of the victory over France in 1871. It was a mixed blessing. The feudal landowning aristocracy lost its dominating position in the country. The explosively expanding factory proletariat, largely made up of former agrarian workers, suffered from abominable working conditions, totally inadequate housing facilities, and starvation wages.

Only the middle class—from which practically all of the expressionist writers, including Georg Heym, sprang—seemed to profit by the industrialization of Germany. It grew prosperous and, for the first time in its history, became the most powerful and influential element in the country. But what the bourgeoisie as a whole gained in authority and prestige in the community, the individual middle-class householder lost in his own environment.

The big cities and new occupations, the entire atmosphere of the modern industrial state, loosened the family ties which had previously kept generations and related branches together as one clan, ruled by a patriarchal figure. The dissolution of these clans robbed the bourgeois of the prospect of becoming such a powerful and respected family head in his own right. He tried to compensate for this loss by doubly asserting his authority over wife and children.[3]

This development had disastrous consequences for the relations between father and son. The father's exaggerated display of domestic authority was naturally aimed mainly at guiding the son's development. This brought to a head the older generation's emotional conflict between the natural desire for their children to be better off than they, and the fear of losing a last vestige of power and prestige once this aim was achieved.

On the other hand, the younger generation, sensing the hollowness of the paternal claim to what seemed "tyrannical" power, displayed even greater rebelliousness than is normal for adolescents. Moreover, the feeling of insecurity underlying the fathers' rearguard action in defense of a way of life which had decayed beyond hope caused the parents to regard all nonconformity, even if purely adolescent and trivial, as a threat to their very existence. In this way they were induced to take up an increasingly stern and repressive attitude toward the younger generation, and so the situation steadily worsened.

The most sensitive, talented adolescents posed a particular problem because they were keenly aware of the situation and reacted more violently than the "average" youth. Moreover, they were capable of giving expression to their feelings and thus lending a voice to the general malaise of their generation. In healthier times the community could well afford the presence of rebellious young poets and philosophers in its organism. The champions of the crumbling Wilhelmian world, however, retaliated against the menace they saw in the behavior of their most gifted sons by ostracizing them.[4]

The father in this way became the symbol of all the restrictive authorities, powers, and traditions which the younger generation encountered. This inflation of the father figure is expressed directly in one of the best known prose works of the expressionist movement. Franz Werfel's words are marked by the exaggerated rhetoric which is characteristic of his style, but which in this instance also conveys the obsessive preoccupation of his generation with the father-son relationship: "What do you mean by—authority of the father?—Everything. Religion: because God is the father of mankind. The state: because the king or the president is the father of the citizens. The law-court: because judges and guards are the fathers of those whom human society chooses to call criminals. The army: because the officer is the father of the soldiers. Industry: because the manufacturer is the father of the laborers."[5]* Franz Werfel was one of the writers of the expressionist generation who, like Franz Kafka, was born beyond the borders of the German Empire. The atmosphere in which these two men grew up and its effect on their personalities were equivalent to those of their German counterparts. Not only were the sociopolitical conditions

---

*In this study all prose quotations are translated. Poetry quotations given only for their documentary value are translated in the text, and the original is given as a footnote. Poetry quoted in a wholly or partly literary context is first given in the original and then in translation in the text. All translations in this study are mine.

in Austria-Hungary very similar to those in Germany, but, moreover, the German-speaking middle class, especially where it was in the minority as in Prague, made every effort to emulate the mode of life of the bourgeoisie in the Reich.

How general the experience of severe friction was between the generations is evident from the unusually large number of books dealing with it which were written in this period. Between 1880 and 1930 approximately as many literary works on the subject appeared as from the beginning of the Middle Ages until 1880.[6] But the writings concerned also show that the father-son relationship was not simply one of pure hatred. Very often, the natural feelings of mutual love and affection would also assert themselves. The clash between these instinctive emotions, on the one hand, and the animosity resulting from the sociological conditions of the period, on the other, could be very painful. Those who experienced it felt that some inexorable power prevented them from obeying the dictates of the heart.

Franz Kafka, for instance, whose attitude toward his father included feelings of insufficiency, hatred, and admiration, explicitly stated in his "Brief an den Vater" that neither of them was responsible for their tense relationship: "I believe that you bear no blame at all for our estrangement. But I am just as completely blameless."[7]

Franz Werfel expressed the same idea in the rhetorical question of the son in his story *Nicht der Mörder, der Ermordete ist schuldig*: "Or are we both confronted by an incomprehensible law that we must *long for* each other *from afar*, and *hate* each other when *together*" (page 137).

Werfel also dealt with the subject in his poem "Vater und Sohn," which depicts the hostile atmosphere pervading the family in such verses as the following:

> Gloomy from angry mealtimes
> their glances meet like steel,
> hostile and vigilant.[*]

In the concluding stanzas of this work, Werfel shows that occasionally the mutual hatred gives way to more positive feelings,

[*]Düster von erbosten Mittagsmählern
Treffen sich die Blicke stählern,
Feindlich und bereit.

generated by the "upsurge of consanguinity" and by a dreamlike
awareness of the boundless love that originally existed between
father and son:

> And the light hand moves toward the old one
> And space seems to convulse
> In miraculous, gentle compassion.*

This ambivalence of the emotional ties of son and father was
also very marked in Georg Heym's case. His family's move to
Berlin in 1900 was in this respect a turning point in his life. At
twelve or thirteen, on the threshold of adolescence, the naïve
childhood world always tends to disintegrate. Values and notions,
which until then are simply uncritically assimilated on the authority of parents and teachers, become questionable. In this process,
the child's absolute faith in his father is, of course, also shaken.

Just at this critical age, Georg Heym was removed from the
sheltered environment of the small provincial towns in which he
had spent his "dreamy" childhood (letter 43). After a brief period
in Posen, he went to Berlin, the most extreme example of the
recently burgeoned industrial metropolis.

In the Imperial capital the disruption of the old pattern of
middle-class life, and therewith the intergeneration tension, had
become more pronounced than elsewhere in the country. Georg
Heym's new environment consequently intensified his normal adolescent tendency toward rebelliousness.

The relationship between him and his father deteriorated. In
the following years, he repeatedly criticized his father for a general

---

*Und die leichte Hand zuckt nach der greisen
Und in einer wunderbaren, leisen
Rührung stürzt der Raum.

Quoted from *Menschheitsdämmerung*. Adolf D. Klarmann points out that
Werfel "was among the first to introduce the father-son conflict into Expressionism," but that he saw the problem "*a priori* in its metaphysical implica-
tions"—"Franz Werfel's Eschatology and Cosmogony," *Modern Language
Quarterly*, VII (1946), 393. Werfel's poem "Vater und Sohn" originally appeared in the collection *Wir Sind*, and is also included in *Gedichte aus dreissig
Jahren* (Stockholm, 1939), pp. 49 ff. Albert Soergel used this poem to contrast
Werfel's ambivalent feelings toward the father with the allegedly completely
negative attitude of Johannes R. Becher in *Dichtung und Dichter der Zeit.
Neue Folge*, pp. 565-66. Curt Hohoff, in reediting Soergel's book, attributed
the poem to Becher and quoted it as evidence of Becher's absolute rejection
of the older generation. Hohoff does preserve the textual inaccuracies of Soergel's quotation. Soergel/Hohoff, II, 476-77.

lack of understanding of his personality, a lack of feeling for art and poetry, and irascibility (2.8.1905, 6.17.1905, 5.25.1906). Such an attitude makes it clear that Georg Heym was under the sway of the spirit of the era, because, in fact, his father did not deserve such criticism. This can be seen from one particular instance, in which Georg claimed that his physical comfort was neglected. He noted in his diary: "My father does not care at all if my hands are frozen, why doesn't he buy me gloves" (4.2.1905). At first sight this might seem a concrete and justifiable grievance, but actually the note is an almost literal quotation from the well-known nineteenth-century novel by the Swiss author Gottfried Keller, *Der grüne Heinrich.*[8] Georg Heym apparently did not have any genuine complaints against his father, and had to borrow from the field of literature to substantiate the criticism which the general atmosphere of intergeneration antagonism demanded from him.

What Hermann Heym really was like is shown by his reactions to a series of incidents which were very characteristic of Georg's behavior, and which, therefore, are worth relating at some length. Early in 1905 Georg had been sent to a small provincial town to continue his schooling. Shortly after his arrival there, he wrote to his best friend in Berlin that he would commit suicide unless he could come to the capital city to see a girl called Nelli Pattison, for whom, just before his departure, he had conceived an immature passion. The friend passed this letter on to Hermann Heym who went to see his son. Georg recorded the interview and what followed in these words: "Quarreled. But reconciled. I promised not to go. Saturday a post-card from Nelli that I should come. I went immediately, regardless of consequences. School-superintendent wires father. Trouble. I say I want to go to Nelli. He lets me go. . . . This time it ended well. But if I cannot go again in two weeks' time, I will again risk my future. Then the affair will probably have a tragic conclusion. But I hope I will be permitted to go" (5.8.1905).

The diary makes no mention of the conclusion of this matter, which, therefore, we may assume to have been settled amicably. Early in the next month the same problem arose anew. On this occasion Georg wanted to join Nelli at a seaside resort on the Baltic coast: "Tomorrow she travels to Rewahl. I wrote her that I would come too, although it is very doubtful that my father will permit this" (6.4.1905). The next day's entry closes with this remark: "My father prohibited me from going, our relations are at breaking point" (6.5.1905).

But although Georg did go to Rewahl for five days, there are no indications that this caused any repercussions. A section of an autobiographical note written less than two weeks later deals with this period and does not contain any reference to acute conflicts (6.17.1905). It may therefore be assumed that Heym's father either revoked his veto or did not react very sternly to Georg's clandestine journey. In any case, it is clear that Hermann Heym exercised his parental authority reasonably and with moderation. This was all the more creditable in view of Georg's highly provocative and refractory behavior, which reflected the combined influence of normal adolescent personality problems and the general father-son friction of his environment.

Nevertheless, these negative tendencies did by no means kill his feelings of filial piety. He was always conscious of an obligation to consider his parents' feelings (10.18.1906, 11.11.1906, 10.16.1907, 5.18.1909), and he specifically acknowledged his father's love (8.8. 1906) and goodness (6.17.1905, 6.10.1908).

The ambivalence of his attitude was for Georg Heym a painful, but insoluble, problem. He longed for cordial relations with his father, but this most elementary impulse was unable to assert itself against the spirit of the age. His despair and perplexity are recorded in a diary note which tries to put part of the blame on the pedestrian milieu of his school: "How I would like to be on better terms with my father, because I can see how much sorrow I cause him, but he cannot understand that I must perish if I do not keep my pride intact in the face of all this pettiness" (5.25.1906).*

The evidence that Georg Heym with part of his mind continued to love and respect his father seems to be contradicted by his last diary entry on the subject. This note contains the following violently abusive and accusatory passage: "I would have become one of the greatest of poets, if I had not had such a swine of a father. At a time when I was in need of understanding encouragement, I had to use all my strength to keep this scoundrel at a distance" (11.3.1911).

*Cf. Franz Kafka in his "Brief an den Vater": "I too have certainly often injured you with my words, but then I was always aware of it, it hurt me, but I could not restrain myself and keep back the word, I regretted it even as I said it."

It is understandable that these words led Helmut Greulich to the conclusion that Georg Heym and his father lived in a state of extreme and unrelieved hostility, for which the latter was to blame.[9] Other commentators have reached similar conclusions.[10] Yet the lines with which the entry opens constitute a serious warning against overestimation of the importance of this outburst. They show that the immediate cause of this attack on his father was Georg Heym's concern over his future reputation as a poet. Although in this way a very specific complexion was put on what follows, Greulich omitted to include this introductory remark in his quotation: "It will later be of great interest to some literary historian to trace my movements. I think that he will find many interesting things. But remember. . . ." The context of this most often quoted remark of Heym's against his father indicates that ulterior motives may have prompted this bitter denunciation. Therefore it does not invalidate the evidence of other more straightforward utterances that his feelings were tragically mixed.

He found himself driven against his will, by forces he did not understand, into a position of antagonism which contrasted sharply with his instincts. In the vital and fundamental matter of his relationship with his father, Georg Heym very early found himself the victim of á blind fate which excluded him from the most natural and necessary community in the world—that of sons and fathers.

2

◌ℑ Schoolboy's Lot

Ⅰɴ ᴛʜᴇ ᴄᴏɴꜰʟɪᴄᴛ between fathers and sons, the older generation
had a very effective weapon in the schools. More than ever, education had become a means for the preservation and continuation of
the Establishment. Even in the 1820's the school was "regarded as
part of the machinery of state and limited to supplying the state
with the necessary number of gentlemen of the cloth, lawyers and
physicians and the like."[1]

This attitude had since then become much more pronounced.
Writing about Austria, where the situation was virtually the same
as in Germany, Stefan Zweig remarked that the state exploited the
school as an instrument for the maintenance of its authority. The
education Zweig received was aimed at instilling in the pupils
an unquestioning acceptance of the existing conditions. The status
quo was depicted as the apex of perfection. The teacher was
supposed to be infallible, the father's utterances incontestable, the
organization of the state absolutely valid for all eternity.[2]

Against this background, it is not surprising that Georg Heym's
experiences as a secondary school pupil were very unhappy ones.
In Berlin he was enrolled at the Joachimthalsche Gymnasium,
which he criticized several years later, in connection with the suicide of a fellow pupil, as the "ruin of all genius" (4.23.1905). He
was not sorry when, after the Easter holidays of the year 1905, he
did not return to this school. Instead he was sent to the small

14

country town of Neu Ruppin, some thirty miles northwest of Berlin. There he boarded at the house of a clergyman, and continued his school career as a pupil of the Friedrich-Wilhelms-Gymnasium.

The reason for the change is not quite clear. Heym had possibly damaged a boat belonging to the Berlin school and was thereupon expelled. It is certain, however, that the banishment to the province was in the nature of a disciplinary action brought about by some act of vandalism.

Under these circumstances it is understandable that from the start Heym would have a very negative approach toward the town of his "exile," as he called it, and toward the Friedrich-Wilhelms-Gymnasium. On the eve of his departure from Berlin he noted in his diary: "I intend to appear in Neu Ruppin as a very outspoken pessimist" (4.23.1905).

Yet not all of his first impressions of his new environment were unfavorable. The principal of the new school at first seemed to Heym to be the type of understanding, sympathetic, fatherly friend he longed to have as a teacher. Unfortunately, he was almost immediately bitterly disappointed and disillusioned. The incident which shattered Heym's optimistic image of Director Begemann is described in a diary entry of June 14, 1906. Full of confidence, Heym had shown his poems to Begemann, but he was completely crushed by the lack of understanding and appreciation he encountered. The director advised him to stop writing poems because, although he showed some imagination, his work was not clear and contained numerous mistakes in spelling and rhythm. Understandably, Heym was of the opinion that Begemann had overlooked the fact that he was still in his formative years.

This occurrence must have taken place within the first weeks after his arrival in Neu Ruppin. In an autobiographical note of the middle of June, 1905, couched in the third person, there is nothing to suggest that Heym's hopes regarding Begemann were still alive. The tone of this entry is, on the contrary, very critical: "His teachers were pedants and peddlers of trivialities who had become dull-witted in the service of the school. He did not find the teacher who could give him the friendship he needed" (6.17. 1905).

During the remainder of his two years in Neu Ruppin, Heym occasionally recorded his opinion about Director Begemann in the most unflattering terms, of which "proletarian of the spirit" was the mildest (6.14.1906). Heym's hatred of the director was based on more than hurt pride. In August, 1906, he drafted a letter to the Provincial School Board in Berlin which contains a number of specific accusations against Begemann. These include the latter's indelicacy in mentioning sexual intercourse to the pupils, his habit of using threats and misrepresentations to browbeat and intimidate both staff and students, and his use of physical force against the latter.

Personal disapproval of his teachers was not the only reason Heym disliked his schools. Both at the Joachimthalsche Gymnasium and at the Friedrich-Wilhelms-Gymnasium, he objected to the substance and method of his courses. These showed a very heavy bias toward the more mechanical aspects of classical philology. In Neu Ruppin, for instance, the weekly schedule of thirty-five compulsory periods included thirteen hours of Latin and Greek— considerably more than a third of the total.[3]

The spirit in which these philological studies were conducted is reflected in a lament Heym made during his first year in Neu Ruppin: "Homer, the schoolmen have taught me to despise you. What would you, Homer, say, if you knew that one who with religious fervor is preparing to become a creative artist must transcribe you like a child copying a primer" (10.31.1905; see also 1.2. 1905, 2.8.1905). For all its childish pathos, this criticism touched on a genuine and severe shortcoming of the educational institutions of the time.

As a rule the instruction was unimaginative and almost calculated to arouse the youths' resentment.[4] One of the pupils who reacted in this way was the later Emperor Wilhelm II, who in his youth attended the top classes of the Gymnasium at Kassel.[5]

But not only those who were subjected to the educational practices of the Wilhelmian Gymnasiums disliked them. The older generation also had its misgivings. Although the conservatism of the schools was a welcome and consciously exploited means of curbing and correcting the adolescents' rebel urges, the prevailing atmosphere in other respects did not suit the middle-class citizens. The tension between their prosperous outward circumstances and the haunting, if probably unconscious, worry over their private status and the stability of their world had led to an escapist attitude. The average German bourgeois tried to hide from the unpleasant realities behind a facade of emotional nationalism.

In the policy statements of the education authorities, this trend was duly acknowledged. The Gymnasium had the task of "training its pupils scientifically and educating them on the basis of piety and love of the fatherland to become diligent and high-minded men."[6]

In practice, the rather ossified humanist traditions of the Gymnasiums tended to set the tone. The resultant air of dryly academic classicism was totally irreconcilable with the nationalistic pathos cultivated by the bourgeoisie. The middle-class criticism of the educational system was formulated in a work by Julius Langbehn entitled *Rembrandt als Erzieher,* which in a short time after its original publication in 1889 went through more than forty editions. Langbehn declared that German art and education should be rooted in the German people's own spiritual and cultural substratum. As he put it, "the German should serve the German Idea."[7] His point of departure was the vaguest possible type of mystical blood-and-soil cult with a Low-German bias. He did not put forward any concrete proposals for improvement of the existing system. Apart from general appeals to German chauvinism, he only offered repeated assurances that Rembrandt's example—as he saw it—provided the cure-all for the ills with which German civilization had been infected by "people wearing real or mental spectacles."[8]

Meanwhile, industry and the universities were pressing for the inclusion of more exact sciences and of German in the secondary-education curriculum. An attempt to meet these demands was made with the school reform of 1892. Because of the conflicting interests involved, it did not produce significant results. A conference which took place in 1900 and enjoyed the active interest and support of Wilhelm II also failed to bring about a solution of the school problem. The demands of the beginning technological age did, to be sure, lead to an increase of modern subject matter in the curricula, but this was not offset by reductions in the traditional fields. Classical languages retained a dominant position.

Being thus increasingly overburdened, the pupils often lost a sense of proportion in their reactions to the misery of their existence. Many were driven to despair; the annual average of suicides among high school students topped fifty.[9]

Georg Heym's diary shows that especially during his sojourn in Neu Ruppin he, too, was dangerously fascinated by the idea of self-destruction.[10] His obsession with suicide plans is certainly a measure of his unhappiness. He suffered deeply under the inadequacies of the educational system, which at the extremely disciplinarian Friedrich-Wilhelms-Gymnasium were probably particularly glaring.

Yet it must not be overlooked that Georg Heym by his own actions made the situation worse than it need have been. His scholarly performance was barely mediocre, and he was repeatedly in trouble on account of drunken escapades (5.25.1906, 6.14.1906). So he exposed himself to much unnecessary unpleasantness, and became responsible for at least some of the harrowing experiences for which he usually blamed his environment.

His school certainly was, on the whole, exceptional. But it was not wholly lacking in redeeming features. The discipline, though undoubtedly severe, was for senior pupils like Heym not uniformly oppressive. They were even allowed to spend some time in approved inns. But this official license did not satisfy all students. Some therefore founded an illegal society called Rhinania.* The school regulations described the activities of this organization as "regular meetings for the purpose of collective drinking bouts etc." and "the imitation of the carousing of university students," and members were threatened with heavy penalties.[11]

Consistent with his generally obstreperous and irresponsible behavior, Georg Heym joined the forbidden society. He undoubtedly did so as a gesture of defiance against his teachers and as a means of expressing his hatred and contempt for them. Although his association with Rhinania apparently did not become known to the school authorities, it had far-reaching unhappy consequences for Heym. A former fellow pupil informed Georg's father, who was very upset by this most serious offence against the school discipline. Until then it had been intended that Georg Heym should study at the University of Heidelberg. He fervently looked forward to this and expected to become a happy man and a great poet there (10.18.1906, 1.3.1907). When his father heard that he belonged to Rhinania, this membership was taken as evidence of his profligacy. As a result it was decided that he should study at Würzburg, where the social life presumably held fewer temptations than at Heidelberg (5.18.1909).

*The name of this society is not to be confused with the student corporation Rhenania, of which Heym was a member during his time in Würzburg.

Georg Heym was extremely disappointed and discouraged by this. Until the end of his life, he repeatedly complained that the decision to send him to Würzburg instead of Heidelberg had robbed him of his only chance of happiness.[12] Ironically enough, he paid this high price for nothing, because he derived no pleasure or satisfaction from Rhinania. When he first came to Neu Ruppin, he noted with approbation that some of the pupils seemed to have an idealistic attitude (5.15.1905). But he soon changed his mind, and expressed nothing but contempt for these "repulsive fellows," who were nothing but "a higher sort of animal" (8.25.1906). The intimate association with them, which was forced upon Heym by the conspiratorial atmosphere of the illegal society, only strengthened his negative opinion. He felt that he debased himself by taking part in their drunken revels (9.4.1905, 12.22.1905). Thus the association with Rhinania only served to emphasize the gulf which separated him from the others. He was, in every respect, the odd man out.

Separated from his family and the acquaintances he had made in Berlin, Heym's lack of rapport with either the teachers or the pupils weighed very heavily on him. He was tormented by the "sorrow of infinite lonesomeness" (10.29.1905), and bitterly complained that he had no one, "not even a dog," to whom he could give his trust or confide his grief (11.6.1905).

The unbearable feeling of isolation sometimes made him try both to hide his dislike of his fellow pupils and to gain their companionship by a show of conformity. But he could not deceive the others by pretending to "belong": "They are aware that it is insincere and exaggerated and that instinctively puts them off" (6. 24.1905). These humiliating, vain attempts at establishing some human contact only worsened his situation and convinced him that his loneliness was irremediable.

His only comfort was the thought that his poetic talent elevated him above the others, while at the same time it exposed him to their surreptitious persecution. This rather paranoid notion is expressed in six verses which do not merit consideration as poetry, but which are highly indicative of his mood:

> Always wear a happy smile:
> Otherwise the damned philistines are glad
> And inject fuel-oil in the wound
> With a great show of pity, of course,

But secretly everyone is pleased
To have nothing in their body but entrails
Full of dung, instead of your flame.[13]

The lack of human contacts in school was all the more serious because there could not be the compensation of cultivating friendships with local girls. Although opportunities for escapades and for sexual intercourse were not lacking, it was quite impossible to establish the sincere and heartfelt kind of relation which would have satisfied Georg Heym's yearning for companionship. Both the social climate in the small provincial town of Neu Ruppin and the school's strict supervision of the pupils' behavior prevented this.

The negative attitude of the Friedrich-Wilhelms-Gymnasium toward the association of its charges with the local girls must be seen in its proper context. In the clash between rebellious youth and reactionary authority, as it took place in the secondary schools, sexual questions played an important part. This was only natural, since at that age the pupils' interest in sexual matters was awakening. Furthermore, the era was characterized by a very general preoccupation with this matter, as is indicated by the theories which Sigmund Freud developed during this time. Freud's hypothesis concerning oedipal instincts, moreover, seemed to give a scientific basis to the fathers' fear of their sons' rebellious intentions, which were linked with the sphere of sexuality.

To combat the development of erotic urges in their charges, the educators, by ignoring the existence of sex, implicitly denied its reality. Where this was not practicable, the whole business was declared to be sinful in the extreme.[14] Stefan Zweig, six years Heym's senior, refers critically in his autobiography to this educational practice and its consequences: "It was this dishonest and unpsychological habit of hushing up and hiding things, which haunted our youth like a nightmare."[15] The elders, who frequently did not practise what they preached, knew only too well that their hypocritical condemnation or suppression would not really dissuade the youths from following the lure of the flesh. They therefore supplemented their pedagogic efforts with strict curbs on the freedom of contact between boys and girls. Prostitution and similar forms of casual intimacy were connived at because they were not considered to undermine the foundations of the bourgeois world. Purely social contacts in the approved forms were welcome as a necessary phase in the perpetuation of the existing order.

But the type of intimate, profound friendship Heym wanted was quite out of the question, because it would have involved better-class girls, without aiming primarily at a socially acceptable union.

The overpowering lonesomeness which was Georg Heym's lot as a schoolboy strengthened the introspective tendencies of his personality. These had been quite marked even before his "exile" to Neu Ruppin. While still in Berlin, in December, 1904, he began to keep a diary for the express purpose of becoming an "ideal spectator of himself" (12.20.1904). His periodic surveys of past failures and achievements indicate that he took this aim very seriously (12.22.1905, 9.14.1906, 10.31.1906).

It may be justified to link his self-reflective urge with the pietist tradition of his Silesian background. The Wilhelmian era was marked by a revival of this type of religious feeling. In these neopietistic currents there flourished a "strong tendency toward self observation and self analysis."[16]

In any case, Heym's introspective bent aggravated the psychological repercussions of the lack of human contacts in Neu Ruppin. He dwelt on his inability to establish the rapport he yearned for, and tried to find the reason for it. A significant part of the blame he put on himself. For example, he had a short-lived hope of gaining the friendship of one of the very few pupils he respected; when this hope was dashed, he reacted by generalizing about his own faults: "It often happens like that to me, that people whom I love very much, and who are attracted by my conversation and my thoughts, soon turn away from me again, repelled by some evil in me" (8.13.1906).

The development of such ideas was further stimulated by the general circumstances of his presence in Neu Ruppin. Having been "exiled" there for some act of vandalism, his surroundings served as a constant reminder of his evil ways. Moreover, the school's restrictive discipline and the mediocrity of teachers and pupils provoked him to ever new transgressions. In his frequent moments of self-criticism, these misdeeds appeared to him as more evidence of his own baseness. The intensive self-reflection could, under these circumstances, hardly fail to lead to dejected feelings of "evilmindedness and impurity" (8.18.1906, 11.11.1906): "I am generally an utterly depraved person and am also mean" (7.25.1906).

Georg Heym's supposed moral insufficiencies were also accentu-

ated in his own mind by the glaring contrast between them and
his passionate love of beauty. He referred to himself as "a scoundrel with a sense of beauty" (2.10.1907), and gloomily commented
on the inconsistency in his character: "To have a deep feeling for
everything beautiful and yet, at the same time, be evil, over-
whelmed by the eternal unfulfilled yearning that finally all beauty
in and around me would come together, and also by the feeling
that my character is totally inadequate, what a desperate fate"
(8.13.1906).

Georg Heym's despondent certainty that beauty would never
manifest itself in and around someone as evil as he reflects the
influence of the Greek ideal of *kalokagathia*. The notion that
"beauty of the soul" manifests itself in the outward appearance had
become part of the phraseological stock-in-trade of the educators
(12.12.1905). Heym attached great importance to it because it
seemed to provide an explanation for his profound unhappiness.
Circumstances had driven him to the belief that his mind was evil.
From this premise he concluded, applying the *kalokagathia* principle in reverse, that he was doomed to live in ugliness. The hold
of these theoretical considerations over his mind was so strong
and his sense of insecurity so great that he became convinced
that he was ugly, although, in fact, he was decidedly handsome.
Even long after he had left Neu Ruppin, he disagreed with the
many people whom he knew to have a favorable opinion about
his appearance (10.10.1909, 3.29.1909). He went so far as to see
the incompatibility of his alleged ugliness and his love of beauty
as the prime cause of his moral inadequacy: "My soul is mutilated
by the discrepancy between my unsatisfied feeling for the beautiful
and my inferior body" (7.10.1906).

At the same time, the idea of being ugly was, in a manner
typical of the insecure adolescent, linked with his inability to find
the human love he longed for. The combined result of these
various notions was that Heym came to regard himself as a victim
of fate, condemned to lifelong unhappiness. He thought his yearning for beauty and his yearning for love were both hopeless, because he had been born ugly. In this way, love was placed in the
same category as the concepts of beauty and virtue, which the
kalokagathia idea made virtually identical.*

---

*In this context it is also noteworthy that on November 27, 1905, Heym,
quoting from memory from Hölderlin's "Emilie vor ihrem Brauttag," changed

Again and again Heym reiterated that love, beauty, and virtue were inseparable aspects of the state of being for which he vainly hoped. His attitude is expressed very clearly in a reference to one of the girls for whom he nursed unrequited feelings: "But I have not become good, because I am not beautiful. If I were beautiful, Goldelse would love me. . . . To be good would be so easy then. One could not help being good, instinctively, out of sheer happiness. But first one has to be beautiful, without beauty there can be no virtue" (9.14.1906; see also 9.10.1905, 12.26.1905).

There was no breaking the vicious circle. Heym's supposed native ugliness made love, beauty, and virtue forever unattainable for him. Often he speculated that if only he were able to find love, he would also become virtuous (11.27.1905, 3.4.1906, 10.5. 1906, 3.15.1908). But he did not seriously entertain this possibility, because the root of his dilemma lay elsewhere—in his supposedly unsatisfactory appearance. If that could be corrected, everything else would right itself. "I could probably still be saved, I would have to be put into a deep sleep, I would have to be made beautiful and strong, I would have to awake in a glade, and then I would have to see beautiful goddesses dancing around me, I would have to see the realm of the blessed. Then I might be redeemed" (4.5.1907).

Sometimes he had a more realistic approach, trying to improve his appearance through exercises. The explicit purpose was to qualify for the love he desired so much. "I am now trying to become beautiful by force, it is really touching how I exert myself to find love" (11.16.1906). But as his ugliness existed only in his imagination, there was no way out of the vicious circle into which he had argued himself. There was no possibility of realizing his longing for beauty, love, and virtue. Fate, by supposedly making him ugly yet giving him a thirst for those things which are only for the beautiful, had condemned him to unending frustration and wretchedness.

---

the original reading, "Denn um die Guten dämmert oft und glänzt ein Kreis von Licht und Lust" to ". . . Licht und Glück." Whereas Hölderlin no doubt used the word "Lust" here in the general sense of "joy," Heym probably unconsciously rejected this word because of its connotation of "carnal lust." To him this was irreconcilable with the idea of the "virtuous," so he substituted "happiness," which to him was practically synonymous with "virtue." Heym also quoted these lines in his diary on September 23, 1906, again with the same change.

When Heym had thus convinced himself that his suffering could never be relieved, he at first thought he was the unhappiest person in the world: "I do not think that there are people who suffer as much as I do" (11.6.1906; see also 10.13.1906, 10.28.1906). Then he found that his fate was not quite unique. He asked the rhetorical question how nature could permit Michelangelo Buonarroti's nasal bone to be broken, so that "a man full of the profoundest sense of the beautiful was forever robbed, not only of the personal feeling of happiness, which always springs from one's own beauty, but also of the happiness of love" (7.21.1906).

With the realization that he was not the only person whom fate had damned to endless wretchedness, Heym's theories seemed to gain objective validity. Herewith a decisive step had been taken in the development of an absolutely fatalistic world view. Heym's trend toward fatalism was further stimulated by his preoccupation with Hölderlin.

In Hölderlin's sojourn at the seminary in Denkendorf, as described in Hans Bethge's biography, Heym cannot have failed to recognize his own situation in Neu Ruppin. In this work, which ranked among Heym's favorite books (7.17.1905), Hölderlin's "life with the less delicately made companions" is described as "unbearable torment." "Sad states of exaggerated excitement and uncontrollable melancholy begin to occur . . . and loneliness becomes the ever more faithful attendant of the deserted one."[17]

The connection between Heym's interest in Hölderlin and the development of his fatalistic outlook on life is confirmed by a quotation which during his second year in Neu Ruppin frequently occurs in the diaries. It is the motto which Hölderlin wrote over his hymn "Fate" ("Das Schiksaal"), and which is an adaptation, possibly by the poet himself, of verse 936 of Aeschylus' *Prometheus*:[18] "Those who worship fate are wise."

Georg Heym never really attained this wisdom. He did not worship fate, but he did recognize it as an incontrovertible and inescapable force guiding the destiny of man. And he attributed it to fate that he, in spite of his fervent wish to partake of beauty, love, and virtue, was excluded from the happy company of the elect.

3

Trial and Failure

AFTER a supplementary examination which forced him to stay in Neu Ruppin two months longer than intended, in March, 1907, Georg Heym gained his leaving certificate from the Friedrich-Wilhelms-Gymnasium. He then matriculated at the University of Würzburg as a law student. His sojourn in Würzburg lasted until the summer of 1908. Following an illness, he went to Berlin, where he spent some months convalescing. During 1909 and 1910 Heym continued his legal studies at the University of Berlin, with a brief interlude at Jena. With some minor interruptions the next year, 1911, was also spent in Berlin. There, on January 16, 1912, in his twenty-fifth year, he drowned in a vain attempt to rescue the only genuine friend he ever had.

Heym's experiences in the not quite five years he lived after leaving Neu Ruppin seemed to vindicate and corroborate the fatalistic outlook on life he had developed there.

The most important instances were connected with love, student life, professional activities, and the world of letters. The events concerned were partly contemporaneous or overlapping, but no purpose would be served by integrating them in one chronological account. What matters is the effect that the series of experiences had in confirming Heym's pessimistic fatalism, not the actual sequence of the occurrences. In the following pages the episodes concerned are therefore related successively, without regard to temporal interrelationships.

Georg Heym, thinking himself physically and mentally unworthy, had all but given up hope of ever winning a woman's sincere love. But shortly after he went to Würzburg, that for which he had so long yearned in vain became reality. He himself had frequently fallen in love, but now, for the first time, he found his feelings reciprocated.

The circumstances of his meeting with Hedy Weissenfels were rather morbid: "In a church, out of which organ music came, the sound of bells and singing. I entered and found love. Then in a cemetery. Happy among the dead" (4.27.1908). But the happiness soon became mixed with doubt and disappointment. The reality of love failed to measure up to his idealized notions. He had thought that his capacity for love was "unlimited," but now he found he could absorb only a certain amount of it, for "excess causes aversion" (6.1.1908).

When he was away from Hedy, he was miserable and longed for her company (5.23.1908, 6.10.1908, 6.25.1908). But when he was with her, he tended to be absorbed by the imperfections of their relationship. He tried to rationalize his feeling of disillusion by blaming the demands of student life on his time, or by accusing Hedy of lacking in the coquetry from which alone "life and its highest manifestation, love," derive their lure. She was "very beautiful, but unskilled in making love" (6.30.1908).

The ambivalence and vacillation expressed in these remarks had marked Heym's relationship with Hedy from the start, as may be seen from his rueful admission that he had been unfaithful to her on the very day he had plighted his troth (6.25.1908). The love affair with Hedy Weissenfels was only a few months old when sickness struck Georg Heym and practically put an end to it. During the month of July he was hospitalized in Würzburg. Upon his discharge he spent an "excited and turbulent" week with Hedy (8.5.1908). Then he went to Berlin. Although he returned for a few more brief visits in November, 1908, his love for Hedy dwindled away rapidly. He declared that he could not bear love, "this bitter love which truly does not make me happy" (8.13.1908). But it was not until the middle of the next year that he definitely admitted he could not force himself to love her any more (6.6. 1909).

The failure of this love affair is to some extent a natural consequence of circumstances beyond anyone's control. Engagements between students and local girls are notoriously precarious. If, after only two months, the association is forcibly interrupted through illness, the prospects are, of course, much worse still. Yet in this particular instance, there may be a little more to it than just bad luck. Heym was naturally upset when he had to go to the hospital (7.2.1908). But he was not completely unprepared. The first signs that all was not well with his health had occurred less than a week after the initial meeting with Hedy (5.2.1908).

Unfortunately, the nature of his illness cannot be ascertained. None of the clinics now in existence in Würzburg possess a record of him. But it is highly likely that the outbreak of his illness (whatever it was) at this particular time was to some extent determined by psychological causes. This would be consistent with his lifelong inability to form satisfactory relationships with members of either sex. It looks as if a fundamental emotional inadequacy made him unconsciously shrink from the realization of his conscious desire for love and friendship. When, as it were by accident, love came his way after all, a mental reaction presumably stimulated the progress of a latent physical ailment in order to escape from the secretly dreaded actualities.

The nature of this inhibition is revealed in the only genuine friendship of his life, with Ernst Balcke. There is an extraordinary fervor in Heym's feelings for this "girlishly bashful" boy,[1] with and for whom he died (8.11.1906, 8.25.1906, 7.1.1908). The true basis of their relation is revealed in a remark he made in Neu Ruppin: "Oh if Ernst were willing, we would become Greeks again, and beauty, untamed grandeur, loneliness would be our gods. And then we would chant our prayers to the setting sun. And how utterly beautiful would it be, if love in the Greek guise were added to it" (3.4.1906). There are also indications that his friend was jealous when Heym betrayed too much interest in girls (1.3.1907).

The development of homoerotic traits in Georg Heym's personality may well have been stimulated by the spirit of the age. However that may be, these traits, once established, aggravated the general problem of his generation. Practically all of his gifted contemporaries were outsiders in the middle-class Wilhelmian society dominated by their fathers. In Heym's case (and other similar or comparable ones) this consequence of the sociological conditions was exacerbated through personal factors. This not only made him even more aware that he did not "belong" anywhere, but it also induced him to put part of the blame on his own physical and moral shortcomings. His abnormal inclinations were to him a concrete manifestation of the forces of fate which had condemned him to agonizing lonesomeness.

In this perspective the affair with Hedy and its failure appear in their full significance. He had always yearned for love as the miracle cure which alone could make him virtuous, beautiful, and happy. His gradually formed conviction that this love was unattainable to him at least unconsciously acknowledged the obstacle which his own nature presented. The association with Hedy represented a last desperate attempt to overcome this cause of his human isolation. It was a rebellion against fate, engendered and made possible by a casual meeting with a girl who was ready to love him.

The termination of the engagement therefore meant much more than merely the end of a youthful infatuation. The failure of the love affair relentlessly drove home to him the spuriousness of any hope to defy fate. With his inability to establish a lasting relationship with Hedy Weissenfels, Georg Heym had to admit defeat in the most auspicious revolt of his life against the fatal forces within and without himself, both of which kept him isolated from his fellow creatures.

The Hedy episode represented a futile attempt by Heym to combat the cause of his lonesomeness insofar as it was of a personal nature. He also tried to alleviate this problem on a more superficial level, by endeavoring to comply with the standards of his environment in his outward behavior.

One such attempt to conform concerned the student corporation. At one time Heym had eagerly looked forward to joining the Heidelberg Vandals, about whom he entertained very romantic notions.[2] When he went to Würzburg instead, he became a member of the student corporation Rhenania at that university. The disappointment concerning Heidelberg gave him from the start a very negative attitude toward Würzburg. It also colored his approach to the corporation which he joined with the feeling of assuming an unpleasant burden (4.25.1907). But no more than a few days after his arrival he had come to the conclusion that the form of social intercourse cultivated in these organizations was more than merely cumbersome, as he had originally feared:

"Corps life is terrible, soul-destroying, idiotic, ludicrous" (5.30. 1907). This was much the same experience as he had had in Neu Ruppin with Rhinania. But there the similarity ends.

Heym's membership in the illegal high school organization was a gesture of defiance toward the world of his teachers and parents. Joining Rhenania was an attempt to conform to the views and standards of his environment. Although his first impressions were highly unfavorable, he persevered for a year and a half in this endeavor to overcome his isolation, at least on the surface, by acting according to the rules and concepts of his class. He not only had to combat his own nonconformist urges in doing so, but was also faced with the antagonism and suspicion of his corporation brothers. As earlier in Neu Ruppin, the others were not fooled by Heym's pretense of "belonging." They could not fail to realize almost immediately that in attitude and loyalty Heym fell far short of their standards. Moreover, his awkwardness in social intercourse often proved to be a source of embarrassment.

In October, 1907, before the affair with Hedy aggravated the difficulties, his position within the corporation had already reached a very critical stage. With tears in his eyes he recorded a revealing incident. At a meeting they had told him, "you are so dull, you keep so aloof. It will never be possible to let you escort a lady when you have become a fully fledged corporation member. You would not be able to entertain her." And Heym defiantly added, "No certainly not! And I am proud that it causes me agony to discuss indifferent things with indifferent girls. I definitely have good reason, my dear fellows, for keeping my distance from you, you nincompoops and fools" (10.19.1907).

Under the circumstances it was inevitable that he should toy with the idea of resigning from Rhenania. But he could not yet bring himself to do so: "Soon it will be time to tread in the footsteps of Nietzsche. Except that it was much easier for him. At home I am surrounded by an environment and by ideas loyal to the student corporation. To break away from that suddenly, to burn all bridges behind me—to be decried as a coward, to be despised everywhere, it would be too much" (10.19.1907).

A letter from his father confirms Georg Heym's remark about the atmosphere of his home being determined by the influence of the student corporation. Cordially, but with fatherly concern, Hermann Heym gave his son advice on how to avoid friction with

Rhenania and on other related matters; in the process he revealed himself to be an active senior member of his own Heidelberg corporation (letter 6).

How closely Georg Heym in this instance identified himself with the world of his father is apparent in his remark that to break with Rhenania would be more difficult than was Nietzsche's resignation from the corporation Frankonia at Bonn University in 1864. Even more indicative of the seriousness with which he regarded this matter is the fact that he remained in Rhenania for another year. Not until November, 1908, when he had been back in Berlin for several months, did Georg Heym resign. He severed his connection with the corporation ostensibly because the constraint was irreconcilable with his love of beauty and freedom (11.2.1908). This was no more than a rationalization, as can be concluded from the fact that he did not seem to rejoice in his regained liberty. His resignation did, as a matter of fact, have a profoundly depressing effect on him (11.7.1908).

This is understandable, because Heym's resignation from Rhenania had a significance far beyond the actual occasion. It provided further evidence of the utter impossibility of adjusting himself to the pattern of behavior current in his environment. Against his individual inclinations he had tried for a year and a half to conform to a tradition which formed the sacrosanct pivot of the academically trained middle-class' existence. Finally he had to recognize the utter hopelessness of this attempt to normalize his relationship with the world around him. With his withdrawal from Rhenania he symbolically acknowledged that he could not escape the fate of being an outsider by pretending to "belong." The entire episode demonstrated once again to him that he was absolutely subjected to the dark powers of fate, "which no human effort makes knowable" (11.7.1908).

Further evidence of Heym's inability to come to terms with the world into which he was born is contained in the story of his legal training and professional activities. His choice of faculty was obviously determined by family tradition and career prospects rather than by his own preferences.

Only one month after he had commenced his studies he expressed his resentment of the legal profession and his contempt for its practitioners: "Since I do not ever want to become a bone-headed lawyer anyway, why do I still wear myself out?" (5.30.

1907). Nevertheless, he did continue his professional training which, if nothing else, did seem to offer one more chance of reconciliation with society. As such, his studies represented the conformist side of his nature. By the same token, his literary activities might be said to manifest his rebel urges. The tension between Heym's desire for social integration and the forces which made him an outsider are reflected in the conflict between his sense of duty concerning his studies and his creative impulse.

These clashed particularly violently after he had left Würzburg. Stimulated by the metropolitan atmosphere of Berlin and lacking the distraction earlier afforded by the Hedy affair, his artistic preoccupation became much stronger. At the same time, to make up for the half year lost with his prolonged illness in 1907, he was forced to pursue his academic work more intensively than before. As a consequence his colliding interests created an insufferable situation: "I come from Byron's biography and am forced to crawl into the dusty mouse-hole of the 'public creed of the land register.' Who understands this change without coming to harm over it" (9.3.1909; see also 9.22.1909).

Toward the end of the following year, 1910, Heym sat for the examination for higher civil service candidates. As this event approached, the pressure of academic work reached its peak. Heym's hatred of it also increased to a hysterical pitch, in which no execration was violent enough to vent his temper. From among many similar notes, the following may serve to illustrate the severity of the clash between law and poetry: "In the morning I sit down at my desk. I open my shit-arse-shit-pig legal shit book, and so it goes for a while, with lowered head through the shit, until I am suddenly forced to write poetry. My power of comprehension for the legal shit is simply exhausted, my brain is long since brimming over with poetic images, and I sit down and write. . . . What if the legal shit be neglected, what if I shit through that lousy shit-pig exam, that is really not so essential—It is much more essential that I remain faithful to myself."[3]

The desire to conform to the traditions of his environment, even at the cost of continued application to the legal profession he loathed, was ultimately defeated. But this outcome was no foregone conclusion, because in spite of his violent dislike of it, Heym persisted in his attempt to embark on a legal career until its obvious failure forced him to give up. He not only passed his examination, but also accepted a legal civil service appointment and during 1911 served for short periods of time at several courts.

However, some months before the date set for his doctoral examination at the University of Rostock in December, 1911, he was compelled to concede the impossibility of bridging the gap between himself and his environment through his profession. He left his legal post in Wusterhausen a.d. Dosse in September with the declared intention of studying Oriental languages to prepare for an interpreter's position with the diplomatic service. This plan was inspired by a desire for travel and adventure, but Heym himself does not seem to have taken the idea very seriously. He was not even sure which languages he wanted to study! (letters and letter drafts 109, 110, 114, 115). Once the project had served to release him from his legal duties, he did not pursue it any further.

But neither did he completely abandon himself to a Bohemian existence. Although he had been forced to renounce all hope of using the legal profession to gain a foothold in the middle-class world, he still did not give up the struggle against the forces which drove him into the position of an outsider. This is clear from the fact that he went ahead with his doctoral examination and, allegedly by less than fair means, scraped through. A doctorate of this nature could only be desirable for reasons of social prestige. Further evidence of his continued desire to be accepted by society is to be found in his plan for changing professions, which was nearing completion when he died. Rather than live as a coffee-house literator, which presumably would have been possible at the price of irrevocable ostracism, he chose to become an army officer.

He had occasionally toyed with this idea before. Toward the end of 1911, he tried to put it into effect with the aid of his father (letters 120, 136). It seems doubtful that he was the right person for a military career; he himself never mentioned the plan in his diaries without expressing skepticism about his aptitude for army life. Even in the earliest relevant note, from the time of the Hedy episode, he was very dubious about the scheme: "Now I want to make up my mind to become an officer. I am quite convinced that I am the most unsuitable person imaginable. So be it" (5.21. 1908).

From the period when he was actually applying for a cadetship comes another note on the subject, in which he sums up his arguments in favor of and those against a military career. The only attractive aspect to him was "the glamor of the outward position (a source of happiness in itself)." As against this he mentioned the drawbacks of an officer's life, "the terrible constraint, the immense expenses, the so-called social intercourse, the superiors, generally the feeling of being subordinate to someone" (9.22.1911).

This ambivalent attitude toward the projected military career reflects Heym's opposing impulses concerning society. The glamorous appearance and the social prominence of the officer's status would have satisfied his yearning to be respectfully accepted by his environment. But at the same time he shuddered at the thought of accepting the limitations of personal freedom which constitute an inevitable part, not only of army life, but of any form of social existence.

Around New Year, 1910, Georg Heym became a member of a literary-philosophical organization. He was accepted on his own merits, and did not have to pretend to conform to views and attitudes which he really could not share. Also, he was not merely granted membership, but was treated with respect and even admired. It might seem that this would at least to some extent have satisfied his longing for social recognition. But actually, his sense of isolation was only increased through his association with this circle. This was due to internal tensions which soon centered around him and his work, and to the nature and composition of the organization.

The Neue Club, in which "the young generation of Berlin poets for the first time came together,"[4] was formed in March, 1909, by the intellectual faction of a Berlin student corporation. Center and initiator of the circle was twenty-three-year-old Kurt Hiller who, since obtaining a doctorate in law two years earlier, had established himself as a man of letters. Around him gathered Erwin Loewenson, Erich Unger, David Baumgardt, Ernst Blass, John Wolfsohn, Robert Jentzsch, Friedrich Schulze-Maizier, Armin Wassermann, and Jakob van Hoddis (Hans Davidsohn). The youngest member Wilhelm Simon Guttmann discovered Heym's talent for the club.

Guttmann wanted to start a progressive theater company and had advertised for dramatic manuscripts. Nothing came of his plans, but Heym submitted a brief one-act play entitled "Atalanta." Guttmann was so impressed by it that he invited Heym to read it to the Neue Club. The same work to which Heym owed his introduction to this organization became the object of a violent controversy among the members. Guttmann still wanted to arrange a performance of the play. His plans were wildly ambitious and far beyond his own or the Neue Club's financial scope. But impractical though his schemes were, their very grandiosity did appeal to Heym's self-esteem. On the other hand Heym was reasonable enough to see that Kurt Hiller's counter-proposal for a very simple performance was much more realistic. So he vacillated between the two plans, thereby heightening the conflict between their respective supporters. It really was a storm in a teacup, because in the end neither project was carried out. But it did place Heym in the center of much intrigue and plotting, and subjected him to exhortations and accusations from both sides.

The conflict prevented his forming any genuine personal attachments to fellow members, and he thus developed a defensive, insecure attitude toward the Neue Club. His situation became even more difficult when he found himself in the center of a much more fundamental controversy among the members. A minority led by Kurt Hiller advocated "cerebral poetry,"[5] the "honest stylization of the thousand small and great delights and sorrows in the experiences of the intellectual city dweller."[6] The first poet to approximate this aim was, according to Hiller, Jakob van Hoddis.[7]

Most of the members were in favor of a more intuitive, emotional type of poetry, for they had a vitalistic-metaphysical outlook on life which contrasted sharply with the rationalism of Hiller and his closer allies. The majority group, led by Erwin Loewenson, was particularly impressed with Heym's primitively natural personality even more than with his work.[8] Heym seemed to embody and epitomize their notions, and thus, he encouraged them to elaborate these views and raise them to the status of a program. This eventually brought the conflict between the factions to a head, and again Heym found himself in the line of fire. He was naturally on the side of those who admired him most, and so he remained in the Neue Club when, early in 1911, Kurt Hiller and his closest friends seceded.

It is clear that the Neue Club did not provide the kind of environment which would have warmed Heym's heart with a feeling of security and coziness. But even apart from its rather bellicose atmosphere, the organization could not have failed to impress further on Heym that he was an outsider. The Neue Club was, after all, an association of antibourgeois, in part even revolutionary elements. In joining this group Heym therefore gained a rather problematical place in a small group at the expense of publicly renouncing his allegiance to established society.

This renunciation was not wholehearted, but rather a sign that the factors which drove him to rebel against the status quo had once again proved stronger than his own conformist urges. That private feelings had to be disregarded when Heym joined the Neue Club is obvious in view of the ethnological complexion of the society. The overwhelming majority of the members were Jewish. Heym must have found this disconcerting, because his background was anything but conducive to the development of philo-Semitic sentiments.

The social and professional status of his parents, his pattern of education, and his family's attachment to the idea of the student corporation all predestined him to share the racial prejudices current among the Wilhelmian bourgeoisie. Anti-Semitic tendencies were, of course, traditional—and not only in Germany, but in the Wilhelmian Empire they had become particularly prominent.

Like the intergenerational conflict and the educational crisis of that era, this vicious anti-Semitism reflected the disrupting influence of the Industrial Revolution of the late nineteenth century on the traditional patterns of thought and life. In this particular instance, the new social standards based on material wealth rather than birth and family amounted to a dissolution of an important aspect of the middle-class world image. Anyone who made enough money could claim admission to the higher strata of society, while the social effects of financial ruin were no longer cushioned by descent and background.

This fluidity of the modern, materialistic society was conceived by the average bourgeois as a threat to his own position. He thus became susceptible to the lure of a racist ideology which filled the gap left by the invalidated scale of values and served to exclude at least one group from social recognition. There was no lack of individuals, parties, and journals prepared to exploit this trend for their own purposes. The latter included the *Gartenlaube*, the symbol of the Wilhelmian bourgeoisie, and it is characteristic of Heym's background that his mother would have liked him to contribute to this particular periodical.[9]

It is therefore not surprising that he thought in terms of racial instinct and was inclined to regard the Jews with hostility. After almost a year of intimate contact with them in the Neue Club, he compared his preconception with his experiences in a manner which is not only indicative of the attitude he had absorbed from his environment, but also reflects favorably on his capacity for self-correction: "My attitude to Jewry is the following: on the basis of racial instinct I am a priori hostile toward it, I cannot change that. But I have become acquainted with so many decent, occasionally even charming representatives of the semitic race (Guttmann, Baumgardt, Wolfsohn), that I have subjected my judgment to a purely rational revision, and that I will not as a matter of course regard the Semites whom I will come to know in future as unsympathetic" (11.14.1910).

That Heym allied himself with an organization consisting almost exclusively of people he disliked "a priori" may be explained partly out of a willingness to exploit any means which might promote his literary career, for he declared: "I only use the Club as a stepping stone."* But calculated opportunism was not the main motive for his association with the Neue Club. The sociological and personal factors which opposed his longing for integration in his own environment created the strongest bond with his fellow members. Their Jewish background accentuated the difficulties which generally hindered the social adjustment of young intellectuals of this generation. Heym's awareness of a common fate was stronger than his racial prejudices. In consciously surmounting the latter he acknowledged that he was incapable of adhering to the ideas of his class. Against his emotions he was driven into the camp of the outsiders.

Georg Heym was constantly torn between a deep-seated desire for the apparent security of a niche in the still intact social façade of Wilhelmian Germany, and irrepressible urges and traits which made conformism impossible. Reluctantly, he was forced into an outsider position which conflicted most painfully with his conscious impulses. He recognized that there were two opposing elements in his personality which, depending on the prevailing mood, he characterized as "realist" and "poet," or as "animal" and "god" respectively (7.16.1905, 10.13.1906, 7.8.1907). Once he made an attempt to explain this duality through his descent from both the

*Friedrich Schulze-Maizier related this in a conversation with this author on October 29, 1960.

"sober Heyms" and the "more refined Taistrzits" (10.26.1906). But basically he regarded himself, without any recourse to genetic theories, as one whom fate had condemned to unrelieved failure, frustration, and unhappiness. Fate—arbitrary, mysterious, and hostile—appeared as the sole force in his conception of the universe. Beside it, there was no place for any principle of divine love and justness: "The good Lord sits up there behind the clouds and does not stir. Everything there is stone, barren hollow and empty.

"Much sooner would the idea of an evil God or an evil fate be possible. Because everything which happens is and becomes evil. Happiness scarcely protrudes from the dust, no more than a minute particle of gold in a desert of sand. Why does the Force always keep hidden, why does It never reveal itself, hmm? Because it is without love, cold and mute like the cloud formations which eternally bear their outstretched heads turned away from the earth, as if they know about a terrible secret and have to carry it with them through all eternity to a dark unknown and distant destination" (6.26.1910).

4

Poetic Preliminaries

THREE STAGES can be distinguished in the development of Georg Heym's talent. These phases mark a gradual modification in the relationship between the writer's personality and his creative work. Initially, writing was a conscious attempt to formulate and externalize moods and emotions. This form of self-expression is typical of the adolescent mind which is subject to frequent and violent emotional upheavals. Bewildered by the mental turmoil, the young person seeks to orientate himself in the labyrinth of his own personality by selecting and recording specific instances of his ever changing feelings and experiences.

This kind of literary activity ceased when Heym reached the level of maturity at which the further development of his personality proceeded less turbulently, and he began to know himself. In contrast to most of those who in early adolescence have literary ambitions and at this stage lose all interest, Heym kept writing.

His creativity entered a second phase, in which the work was no longer primarily a manifestation of the yet unknown, puzzling self, no longer a signpost for his own guidance in the exploration of the self. At this level he came to regard his writing mainly as a demonstration of his literary-technical skill, which was to inform the world of his talent. The subject matter was no longer taken from the panorama of the inner self, but from any external impulse which stimulated the form-giving abilities. This did not mean that the creative work henceforth was entirely objective in nature, but only that the former direct subjectivity was replaced by indirect subjectivity. The world was perceived from a highly subjective viewpoint, so that it actually seemed to reflect Heym's fluctuating but predominantly somber moods.[1]

In this way the literary treatment of externals still involved the writer's private moods. Only when this phase too had passed and Heym's creative talent really and fully matured did personal experiences and emotions cease to intrude upon the work. The full deployment of his creativity was marked by the sublimation of all private feelings to the level of a universal existential principle. In this phase the work was neither a direct record of mental states nor the stylization of subjectively tinged impressions, but the expression of a comprehensive conception of the universe. The gradual loosening of the ties between Georg Heym's private life and his writings will in the following pages be traced through these three phases.

Georg Heym's initial attitude to his literary attempts is characterized by the equation of "pure creation" with "pure enjoyment" (4.12.1906). He wrote because it gave him personal pleasure and satisfaction to do so. In this earliest phase he wrote practically only poetry, a genre so often mistakenly believed to be the ideal vehicle for outpourings of the soul. That Heym in this period reveled in versification for this reason is clear from the direct subjectivity of the texts concerned.

His predominant mood of despondency is mirrored in immature verses which are completely lacking in artistic value. An example of these poems is "Complaint" ("Klage"), from 1903:

> Ich kann nicht mehr singen
> Mir ist so bang.
> Ein leises Verklingen
> Nur zu mir drang
>
> Von einem Kuss,
> Den sie mir hingehaucht,
> Ein Duft von ihrem Haar,
> Vorbei, verrauscht.
> Einem andern bot
> Sie sich dar.
>
> Ich hab am Felsen die Leier zerschellt,
> Die ich rührte zu ihrer Ehre.

Ihr schrilles Ächzen die Lüfte durchgellt.
Ich schau ihr nach und blicke ins Leere.*

(I can sing no more
I am so afraid.
Only an echo
softly reached me

Of a kiss,
Which she breathed on me,
A fragrance of her hair,
finished, faded out.
She gave herself
To another.

On the rock I smashed the lyre,
Which I struck to her glory.
Its sharp sigh pierces the air.
I look for her and see emptiness.)

This poetic endeavor directly links Heym's private experiences with his creative ability, and indicates the subjectivity of his literary approach. The idea that his unhappy existence might have a pernicious influence on his talent is also found repeatedly in the early diaries. A poem quoted on June 14, 1905, ends thus:

O Sehnsucht, die in Qualen sich auf
lichtgemiednem Lager windet,
—Einst kommt der Tag, der Dich
verhungert und verdürstet findet.

(O Yearning, which in sorrow writhes
on an ever gloomy couch
—The day will come which finds you
perished for lack of sustenance.)

A few months later Heym noted in his diary that he lived in fear that his "poetic vein would have to dry up for lack of great happiness or great sorrow." The same entry contains a poem dealing with this idea which ends as follows:

*Heym's poetry is quoted from Vol. I of *Dichtungen und Schriften.*

Dann, vergessend in der innern Ode,
dass einst frisch das Herz geschlagen habe,
Ist ein Mensch der Nessel gleich, die schnöde
Wuchert über seinem eigenen Grabe.   (9.4.1905)

(Then, forgetting in the inner barrenness
that once his heart beat boldly,
Man is like a nettle which basely
Luxuriates on his own grave.)

In this connection it is interesting to note that the first time Heym referred to his poetic talent in his diaries, it was to complain that the misery of his existence had robbed him of his creative powers. Reminiscing about previous poetic achievements he wrote: "As far as poetry is concerned my brain is squeezed just as dry as any old lemon. That is due to the fact that I never really experience any happiness with which I can fortify myself" (4.2. 1905).

Other examples of the close and immediate connection between Heym's early literary attempts and his private moods and pre-occupations concern Hölderlin. One of the youthful Heym's first versified references to this poet, whose life and works deeply impressed him, is highly indicative of the subjective, cerebral nature of the poetry of this period.

Einsam über Hügel ging ich
Durch den lichten, blauen Abend,
Sah im West die Sonne sinken,
Hinter Hügeln untergehen,
Und ich dachte an Hölderlin.

(Lonesome over hills I went
Through the clear, blue evening,
Saw the sun set in the west,
Going down behind the hills,
And I thought of Hölderlin.)

The autobiographical use of the personal pronoun "I," completely lacking in the mature poetry, occurs twice in these five lines. The turn of phrase "I thought" would be especially unthinkable in the context of the later works.

Hölderlin stimulated the development of Heym's fatalistic world view in the Neu Ruppin period. Heym repeatedly quoted and paraphrased "Hyperion's Song of Fate" ("Hyperions Schicksalslied") in the diaries. He also used it as a model for a poem. Heym's verses embody the obsessive notion of his own ugliness and abandonment by the gods to unending misery. The second stanza links the notions of beauty, happiness, and virtue in conformity with the theoretical vicious circle on which his fatalism was originally based.

Die Hässlichen

Die Verstossnen hören die Götter nicht
Und voll Ekel wendet der Gott sich ab,
Wenn der Kinder der Nacht
Eines wimmert im Jammerlaut.

Denn die Götter hören die Schönen nur,
Diese wandeln herrlich den Sonnenpfad
Selber dem Göttlichen gleich
Immer gut und sich selbst genug.

(The Ugly Ones

The gods do not hear those who are cast out
And full of disgust God turns away
When one of the children of darkness
Whimpers plaintively.

For the gods only hear the beautiful ones,
They walk splendidly on the path of the sun
Themselves godlike
Always virtuous and contented.)

Their pronounced direct subjectivity is, of course, not the only thing which distinguishes the efforts of the first phase from later work. There is also, inevitably, a very marked difference in the technical level of achievement. Heym's development as a poet in this respect can be gauged by juxtaposing some of his early products with later ones on comparable subjects.* The earliest

*The negative comments made on the early poems of Georg Heym only serve to indicate his subsequent growth in artistic stature. There is no point in critically analyzing for their own sake a child's lyric attempts which reflect in no way on his later achievements.

preserved poem by Heym dates from 1899, when he was twelve years old.

Die Quelle

Aus der Quelle
Rinnet helle
Eines Bächleins klare Flut.

Es ergiesst sich,
Überschiesst sich
In der heissen Sonnenglut

Niemals weilend
Lustig eilend
Übers schroffe Felsgestein,

Zischend, sausend
Donnernd, brausend
Stürzt sichs in die Kluft hinein.

(The Spring

From the spring
Runs brightly
The clear water of a brook.

It pours out
And tumbles about
In the hot glow of the sun,

Never tarrying
Gaily hurrying
Over the rough rocks and stones,

Hissing, rushing
Thundering, splashing
It plunges into the abyss.)

By the unrelieved regularity of rhythm and rhyme these verses immediately reveal themselves as the product of earnest but uninspired endeavor. There is a logical flaw in the fact that the stream, which in the first three stanzas is described in terms suggestive of smallness, in the last one, without transition, turns into a raging cataract. Poetically this leads to a fatal inconsistency between content and the light, playful meter.

Since Heym in his mature poetry avoided such breaks, the objects of comparison for the two parts of "The Spring" must be taken from different sources. For the description of the dainty stream in stanzas 1-3, the third stanza of "Corpus Christi Procession" ("Fronleichnamsprozession"), from 1910, provides a suitable pendant.

> Des Feldwegs Brücke steigt im halben Bogen,
> Wo helle Wellen weisse Kiesel feuchten.
> Die Wassergräser werden fortgezogen,
> Die in der Sonne aus dem Bache leuchten.

> (The path's bridge rises in a semicircle,
> Where clear waves moisten the white gravel.
> The waterferns are washed along,
> Which in the sunlight sparkle in the brook.)

The superiority of these verses over the earlier ones is particularly evident in the substitution of visual images for descriptive adjectives and adverbs. In "The Spring" the water is merely described as "clear." In "Corpus Christi Procession" the whiteness of the gravel on the bottom is visible, and the submerged weeds reflect the sunlight, demonstrating the clearness of the stream in visual terms.

Similarly, in the early work, the movement of the water is described in a number of rather stereotyped verbs, whereas in the other the current manifests itself in its effect, as it washes the weeds along. The unity of the scene in "Corpus Christi Procession" is stressed through the image of the water's moistening effect on the gravel it runs over. In "The Spring" this integration of the poetic image is lacking.

The cataract stanza of "The Spring" can be compared with the second quatrain from "Styx" (1910).

> Entsetzlich wälzt sich hin der Phlegeton.
> Wie tausend Niagaras hallt sein Brüllen.
> Die Klüfte wanken von den Schreien schon,
> Die im Orkan die Feuerfluten füllen.

> (Terrifyingly the Phlegethon rolls along.
> Like a thousand Niagaras its roar resounds.
> The chasms start to waver from the cries,
> Which fill the fiery waters in the tempest.)

Again the mere enumeration of the waterfall's qualities has been replaced by a number of highly expressive verbs and metaphors.

An equally important advance in poetic treatment of the cataract motif is the substitution of heavy iambic tetrameters for the trochaic two- and four-footers.

Both the loss of the initial egocentricity and the development of the technical aspects of Heym's talent can be demonstrated with the aid of another pair of poems.

Mitternacht

Nacht ists! Die schwarzen Wolken jagen,
Vom Sturm gepeitscht, hin in den Mond, den blassen,
Und schwere Tropfen niederschlagen.
Ach, ich kann sie nicht durchdringen
Die ewig schwarz die Welt umschlingen.
Wo ist die Wahrheit, wo das Licht,
Des Abglanz doch nur durch die Wolken bricht?*

(Midnight

It's night! The black clouds rush,
Lashed by the wind, into the moon, the pale one,
And heavy drops begin to spatter.
O, I cannot penetrate them,
Eternally shrouding the world in black.
Where is Truth, where is the light
Whose reflection only breaks through the clouds?)

The main weakness in the structure of this text is the lack of integration between the nature description in the first lines and the philosophic despair at being unable to perceive Truth, which is professed in the last four verses.

A stormy night and the loss of truth are also the subject of stanza four of the later poem, "The Infernal Eucharist" ("Das infernalische Abendmahl"—1911) which depicts the beginning of a cathedral's desecration by the iniquitous rite.

---

*This poem is quoted from Greulich, p. 43; the variant published in *Dichtungen und Schriften*, I, while basically identical, is probably corrupted, as indicated by the (strictly speaking) meaningless concluding lines: "Gibt es denn Wahrheit? Ist denn Licht,/ Des Abglanz nur durch Wolken bricht." Since the apparatus is not available, the editor's reasons for preferring this version over the superior one printed by Greulich are not known. But even if the authenticity of the Greulich text should be dubious, it is usable for the purpose of illustrating the degree of subjectivity of Heym's poetry at this stage, since the two versions do not differ in substance.

Nachtschwarze Wolken drängen in den Dom
Voll Sturm und Blitzen durch das grosse Tor.
Ein Wetter tost. Im schwarzen Regenstrom
Versinkt der Orgel Ton im fernen Chor.

(Night-black clouds surge into the church
Through the big gate, replete with storm and lightning.
A storm rages. In the black downpour
The organ tone sinks in the distant choir.)

The exclamatory style of the first three verses in the early poem
prevents them from achieving the menacing effect of the comparable image from "The Infernal Eucharist." The change in poetic
approach which took place between these two poems is very
obvious when their differing thematic contents are juxtaposed.
"Midnight" gives a completely abstract formulation of some fit
of adolescent despair, undisguisedly autobiographical and private.
In "The Infernal Eucharist," on the other hand, the intrusion of
the forces of darkness which conceal truth is presented as a
suprapersonal phenomenon, and is couched in the concrete image
of the teeming rain drowning out the sound of the organ, which is
the symbol of true religion.

The first, self-exploratory phase in Georg Heym's literary development came to an end in the summer of 1906. At that time,
quite suddenly, his creative attitude changed completely. Heym's
reflection on this is in terms which show that the transition to the
second stage of his writing career happened altogether involuntarily: "Briefly one thought which occurred to me today. I used to
make my poems out of unclear inner moods which in my mind
crystallized into poems. They were all in me for quite a time, I
felt them in me, before I could form them. Today it struck me
that I created the two poems which I made today, also that of
yesterday, only out of a sudden, accidental appearance before my
eyes of their subject matter, their contents. Yesterday I saw a
branch laden with fruit, today I suddenly heard the rain on the
trees, then I saw the vine pushing up through the earth. As if of
their own accord three poems resulted from this. But it used to be
more beautiful when I had to struggle with myself" (8.26.1906).

The formulation of this note, with the juxtaposition of the "unclear inner moods" as the origin of the earlier poems and the
"appearance of their subject matter, their contents" as the basis

of the later ones, leaves no doubt about the nature of the change. It was a transition from a completely egocentric phase of literary creativity to one in which the skill in stylizing external impressions was stressed. The aspects in which Heym's new approach to writing differed from the old are specified in notes from the period following the transition.

In one of these he rejected his earlier theories about the effect of happiness or the lack of it on the creative capacity. Instead, he maintained that the author's moods have no bearing on his art: "I used to say only when you are happy you can work. Then also: it goes best when you are unhappy. Now: art is something which is outside man. It has absolutely nothing to do with moods. The inexplicable must simply be worshiped" (9.22.1907, 8.25.1906).

Whereas this note deals with the loss of the initial tendency toward versified soul-searching, another is concerned with the change in emphasis from content toward form: "It is easy to have imagination. But how difficult to formulate its images" (9.20.1908). The display of poetic skill was, for the insecure adolescent who in this period became increasingly conscious of being almost totally isolated from the rest of humanity, a means of gaining admiration and recognition from his environment. He no longer wrote for his purely personal pleasure and satisfaction, but for a public whose applause and respect he coveted. Consequently, soon after the change in his creative attitude took place, he began to consider the possibility of having his work published. As he put it, he wrote to the minor poet and story-writer J. J. Horschik, "a letter, which can give me much."*

*Diary entry made between November 25 and 27, 1906. Heym contradicted himself in the entry of January 3, 1907, according to which an acquaintance wrote the letter. However that may have been, the object was to persuade Horschik to promote Heym as a poet. Josef Johann Horschik was born on February 16, 1874, in Schönhof bei Podersam (Bohemia) and lived in Dresden as a businessman. In 1905 he published a collection of poetry *Lieder des Wanderers,* and in the following year the novella *Reif im Frühling.* These publications may have looked like the beginning of a promising literary career and may have given Horschik a short-lived reputation in the realm of letters. Otherwise Heym's selection of him as a sponsor is hard to understand, although Horschik's Bohemian origin and synthesis of literature and prosperity may also have appealed to the materially and artistically ambitious young Silesian. Whatever expectations Horschik may have aroused with his first works were subsequently disappointed. In spite of a novel (*Johannes Lister,* 1908), and more poetry (*Unter Sternen,* 1936, and *Sudetenland,* 1940), he is insignificant as an author.

The recipient's initial reaction was apparently quite encouraging, because about a month later Heym noted that Horschik was prepared to look through his poems and send them on to another man of letters (1.3.1907). In the hopeful mood aroused by this promise, Heym revealed his main reason for all this maneuvering. If the poems were printed, he could send a copy to a girl he hardly knew, but for whom he had conceived a hopeless passion. This evidence of his creative talent was to compensate for his supposed inadequacies, and to make him worthy of love. Here is a clear indication of the complete transformation of his attitude, from self-reflection to public-minded self-advertisement.

But the attempt to enlist Horschik's assistance in finding a publisher failed. His next letter was a great disappointment for Heym: "I would be a fool if I were to let Horschik's letter annoy me. What he advises, I will certainly do. 'In spite of my irritation there is something in your poems which compels me to keep you in mind.' Pompous nonsense. 'Your poems contain philosophical problems, have you thought them through?' Fate, they don't believe that one can suffer from you so young. But the letter will be carefully preserved" (1.23.1907).

During the following Easter vacation Heym made another vain attempt to persuade an established man of letters to take up his cause. He visited the literary theorist Wilhelm Bölsche, and although this step had no immediate consequences, he hoped the contact might later prove useful (5.23.1907). He therefore intended to look up Bölsche again during his next holidays (6.6.1907). After this, there is no further mention of Bölsche in the diaries, nor is there any evidence to suggest that there was any further contact between him and Heym. It is impossible to detect any literary or human affinity between them. The selection of such an incommensurable but well-known figure as promoter indicates that at this stage Heym's only aim was to be presented as a poet to the widest possible public, even at the price of betraying his talent.

In a different context, this readiness to make artistic sacrifices for the sake of publicity had very far-reaching consequences. Still associating lyric poetry with the subjectivity which he had meanwhile discarded, Heym adopted another genre which was incompatible with the essence of his talent, but which by its very nature is directed at a public: the drama.

Naturally, the thought of writing a play had occurred to him before. As early as October, 1905, on his eighteenth birthday, he conceived the plan for a drama dealing with the twelfth-century Italian schismatic priest Arnold of Brescia (10.31.1905). But it is significant that this project was not mentioned again until a year later, shortly after the second phase in Heym's writing career had commenced (10.13.1906).

From then on, "Arnold of Brescia" ("Arnold von Brescia") and other dramatic attempts replaced lyric poetry as his favorite medium of literary expression. This bias prevailed during the approximately three years of this stage of his development. Only during the heyday of his relationship with Hedy Weissenfels was there an interruption. When it seemed as if the ultimate aim of his writing —to break through his social isolation by reaching a public—had been forestalled by the fortuitous finding of love, the literary efforts were abandoned, for in spring and early summer of 1908, Heym apparently wrote only a few poems for Hedy.

Heym's disenchantment with the Hedy affair after his return to Berlin is reflected in a renewal of his interest in writing (9.13.1908). And when the love affair had virtually run its course, Heym became completely engrossed again in the dramatic projects that had been shelved during his association with her (1.9.1909). Writing again became a means of seeking the social recognition and acclaim which he desired. Heym's strong interest in this all-important problem made the success or failure of his literary attempts of vital concern.

The play about Arnold of Brescia caused him many moments of anxiety. Sometimes he felt that he had overreached himself in the choice of subject matter, and complained that he could not cope with it because it was much too big for him (10.13.1906). At other times Heym put the blame for his failure on the circumstances rather than on his own inadequacies, and lamented that he could not succeed because he had no sources or appropriate reference works at his disposal (10.16.1906).

These moods of despair alternated with optimistic phases in which Heym was full of hope regarding his work and his talents. In one note, in which he actually remarked on this alternation of his moods, he stated explicitly that he regarded the play as a vehicle for attaining the fame he yearned for, and then indicated how far the work had progressed: "In me alternate enthusiasm

and disgust, faith in myself and self despair. And yet, if at this
early stage I managed to become immortal through 'Arnold of
Brescia.' One year has passed since the work was started, the plan
is just about complete, but it seems to me there is still so much
lacking in the way of connecting and incidental scenes, which
must bring Brescia to life" (10.31.1906). A week later he was very
pessimistic again: "I despair of my poetic vocation" (11.6.1906).
Thus fluctuating between confidence and despondency it was more
than a year later before Heym finally and definitely admitted defeat in the matter of "Arnold of Brescia." Early in 1908, he felt
that he had gone hopelessly astray in the subject matter, and
definitely renounced the project (1.19.1908).

He may well have resigned himself to the failure of "Arnold
of Brescia" at this time, because meanwhile he had become increasingly preoccupied with another play. In the autumn of 1907,
Heym resumed work on a fragment dating back to his Neu Ruppin
school days. This fact is apparent from a diary entry of late
September: "Maybe this should be recorded: the 'Sicily Campaign'
written in four days. Accidentally I came upon the sheet on which
I once in Neu Ruppin had noted the beginning of the dialog
between Alcibiades and Socrates. It fascinates me immediately
and I write. When I did not know how to go on, suddenly a
thought came to me" (9.22.1907).

After a week the first enthusiasm about this sudden rush of
inspiration had died down enough to enable the author to make a
more critical evaluation of his work. It appeared to be still far from
perfect and complete. Heym mildly denounced himself for being
content with the first act, while revealing that the other acts
were not yet developed because he was still too firmly under the
sway of Grabbe's style to write anything but a pastiche of his
work (9.30.1907). However, in the following weeks he did bring
the play to a conclusion, and before the year was out it was
privately printed under the title "The Athenians' Excursion" ("Der
Athener Ausfahrt").*

---

*Both Heinrich Ellermann, in "Georg Heym, Ernst Stadler, Georg Trakl.
Drei Frühvollendete. Versuch einer geistesgeschichtlichen Bibliographie,"
Imprimatur. Ein Jahrbuch für Bücherfreunde (Hamburg, 1934), V, 158 ff., and
Hans Bolliger, in his bibliography appended to Seelig's *Gesammelte Gedichte*,
list among Heym's published books *Der Athener Ausfahrt. Trauerspiel in 1.
Aufzug* (Würzburg: Memminger, 1907). I have not been able to inspect a copy
of this book.

The publication of "The Athenians' Excursion" must undoubtedly have had a favorable effect on Heym's self-esteem. It also opened up the possibility he had toyed with early in the year in connection with attempts to publish his poems. He could now try to bring himself to the attention of the girl of his dreams through his literary work (12.27.1907). For this purpose a drama set in ancient Greece was, of course, just as suitable as a play about a twelfth-century priest. Consequently Heym felt that he could afford to scrap "Arnold of Brescia" as a rather hopeless undertaking. However, the publication of "The Athenians' Excursion" did not have the desired result, as Heym's hopes regarding the girl he was infatuated with failed to materialize. But this did not discourage him from continuing his dramatic efforts.

In the months that followed the publication of "The Athenians' Excursion" and the renunciation of "Arnold of Brescia," he occupied himself with a number of dramatic projects, dealing with such subjects as Spartacus, Catilina, and Jugurtha. The most important of these was a one-act play called "The Wedding of Bartolomeo Ruggieri" ("Die Hochzeit des Bartolomeo Ruggieri").

Out of this grew subsequently his most successful drama, "Atalanta," which gained him an introduction to the world of letters as represented by the Neue Club. The first version of "The Wedding of Bartolomeo Ruggieri" was written in twenty-four hours, a few weeks before the meeting with Hedy which put a temporary halt to his literary activities (4.3.1908).

Heym did not forget "The Athenians' Excursion" with all of these new dramatic projects, nor did he give up hope of reaching the public with it. Early in 1909 he still dreamed of becoming famous through the play. He visualized the scene in the theater when the audience would acclaim him as a genius: "I often imagine how it will be when the curtain has fallen over Alcibiades' corpse. How the people will then cheer and acclaim me" (4.11.1909). Heym did not limit himself to wishful thinking. Early in the summer of 1909 he approached Maximilian Harden, the most famous and influential journalist of the time. Heym obviously wanted to get the play reviewed in Harden's widely read literary and political weekly journal *The Future* (*Die Zukunft*). He attached great importance to the outcome of this step, which he thought would be decisive for his literary career (6.6.1909). A month after Heym had given Harden the play, he received an encouraging reply from him: "I just received the reply from Harden. He has read the 'Excursion.' He finds many traces of a nice talent in it. He will soon invite me, when he is less busy. Is my star about to rise?" (7.7.1909). But once more, nothing came of his plans for finding a promoter for his literary career, and there is no indication that Harden kept his promise of an invitation.

Although the work of this second phase of Georg Heym's literary career was primarily intended as a public display of his creative gifts, in which the subject matter as such was without great importance or personal relevance, there is still considerable indirect subjectivity in these writings. This can be seen even in the poems, few in number and seemingly purely descriptive, which he wrote during his romance with Hedy. She shared his delight in the beauties of nature as together they explored the surroundings of Würzburg. Impressions from these walks sometimes provided the inspiration for his brief lyrical sketches.

A diary entry of June 13, 1908, describing an outing from which they had just returned, includes two stanzas which contain a good description of a sudden thunderstorm striking the country.

> Die nahen Donner schallten von dem Fluss
> der Wind ergriff der Inselpappel Laub
> und warfs dem Ufer zu als Herbstesgruss
> die Strasse lang erhob sich grauer Staub.
>
> Die Vögel flohen ihrer Nistung Schutz
> unsicher flatternd über dunkler Flur
> Ein Falke nur bot drohndem Sturme Trutz
> und zog gelassen seine runde Spur.
>
> (The nearby thunder sounded from the river
> wind grabbed the island-poplar's leaves
> and threw them to the shore as autumn greeting
> along the street gray dust blew up.
>
> The birds fled from the safety of their nests
> fluttering uncertainly over the dark ground
> Only a falcon braved the menacing storm
> and continued calmly his circular trail.)

In the same diary entry Heym recorded that every morning they brought home a veritable forest of poppies and dog roses. He

then added a poetic description of Hedy picking an abundance
of these flowers.

Roten Mohnes Blüten nahmst du viele.
Schöne Blumen, die der Sommer gab.
Brachst mit feiner Hand die feinen Stiele
Aus der Woge grüner Garben ab.

In die Schluchten hingen Rosen nieder,
Die sich willig deinem Wunsche boten,
Glänzten in den hohen Farben wieder,
Da sie nun an deinem Herzen lohten.

(You took many blossoms of red poppies.
Pretty flowers which the summer gave.
Broke with delicate hand the delicate stems
From the wave of green plants.

Roses hung down in the gullies,
Which were willing to obey your wish,
Shone again in high colors,
Now that they blazed against your heart.)

It may here be pointed out that these two poems with their
genuine, stylistic sensitivity, in comparison with his earlier efforts,
bear witness to the development of Georg Heym's lyric talent.
Significant in this connection is the skill with which the type of
rhyme employed in the respective poems matches the atmosphere
evoked by their contents. In the first poem the threatening force
of the thunderstorm, which tosses the leaves and dust up in the
air and causes unrest among the birds, is fittingly connected with
the short, abrupt, masculine rhymes, three out of four of which
symbolize the mood of nature in their dark *u* sound. The iambic
meter further strengthens the ominous effect of this poem. In the
second poem lighter vowels set the tone throughout. The pre-
dominance of feminine rhymes and the trochaic meter are of great
value in capturing the festive summer atmosphere of the scene.

A subjective element is obviously the basis for the difference
in spirit between these two poems written on the same day. Their
respective moods represent the poles of ominous gloom and light-
hearted happiness between which Heym vacillated in these months
of "bitter love." But in the first of these poems there is also a much

more significant instance of self-revelation to be found. To demonstrate this, it is necessary to consider first another poem which Heym wrote during the week after his discharge from the hospital and before his departure from Würzburg. Heym and Hedy walked the same way they had taken earlier in the year, and again Heym summarized the scenery in a short poem.

Tod des Sommers, da die Sicheln blinken
auf der Flur und schon die goldnen Garben
von der Schnitter Schlag in Schwaden sinken
und des Sommers bunte Blumen starben.

Einst war Frühling hier da noch dem Pfluge
unsre Augen folgten bis zum Rande
und der heimwärts ziehnden Vögel Zuge
über Wald und Tal im kühlen Lande

Zeit der Lese, da sie Kränze winden
Aus den Ähren, die wir reifen sahen
Und wir wissen Worte nicht zu finden,
Wo des Herbstes Trauer will uns nahen.   (7.31.1908)

(Death of summer, as the scythes shine
in the fields and golden sheaves begin
to fall in swaths from the mower's stroke
and the bright flowers of summer died.

Once spring was here when our eyes still
followed the plow until the edge
and the flocks of birds returning home
over forest and valley in the cool land.

Harvest time when they bind wreaths
From the ears, which we saw ripen
And we cannot find words,
Because the sadness of autumn is upon us.)

The three stanzas lament the death of summer and are penetrated by an autumnal feeling of decline and retrospection. As the work was written at the very height of summer, the last day of July, the landscape described by Heym is determined more by his own sadness at the prospective parting than by objective observation. The anticipation of autumn obviously reflects his feeling that the end of the affair, and all it implied, was inevitably at hand. This conclusion lends considerable significance to the image in stanza one of the first of the earlier poems, in which the leaves blown from a tree are called an "autumn greeting." In a poem from the middle of June, this expression is very premature. At that time, moreover, it still appeared as if Heym and Hedy had many months of undisturbed companionship ahead of them, and the state of the affair was as auspicious as ever. But in the light of the later poem, the untimely introduction of the autumn motif may be interpreted as a sign that Heym was even then darkly aware that the attempt to end his isolation through love was doomed. The poem implies that Heym, even when his romance was in its most promising stage, was depressed by a premonition of inevitable failure. In this respect, these verses complement the fact that the illness which put an effective end to his association with Hedy first announced itself only one week after he met her. In contrast to the poems of the earliest phase of Heym's literary development, which intentionally attempted to reflect his emotions, this work from the second phase thus involuntarily revealed his innermost mind.

5

Heroes Without Hybris

GEORG HEYM's dramatic attempts also reveal the indirect subjectivity typical of the transitory phase between egocentric soul-searching and mature writing. To demonstrate this only those plays will be cited which he regarded as completed. No conclusions can legitimately be drawn from the many fragments he left.*

The only completed dramas are those of which the final versions are called "The Sicily Campaign" ("Der Feldzug nach Sizilien") and "Atalanta." The former of these works, which Heym vainly tried to get published at the end of 1909 (letter 11), was at various times also referred to as "The Athenians' Excursion." "Atalanta" was the designation applied to the later versions of "The Wedding of Bartolomeo Ruggieri" which Heym wrote during and after 1909.†

Both plays reveal that Heym, in his second phase as a writer, had the same attitude toward historical and literary source material as he displayed toward nature scenes in the Hedy poems. These dramas, too, reflect his own preoccupations and personal problems in the treatment of the subject matter. In "The Sicily Campaign" Heym's overpowering feelings of homelessness and

*Dichtungen und Schriften, II. It is frankly hard to see what purpose is served by the publication of all these bits and pieces. A writer should be judged on his works, not on his wastebasket.

†It is not clear why in Dichtungen und Schriften, II, two versions of this work under these respective titles are published as if they were separate plays.

helplessness have, somewhat inappropriately, been attached to the figure of Alcibiades. At the same time, this character represents Heym's adolescent ideal of the beautiful, brave, reckless, and irresistible young man. In the tense relationship between Alcibiades and the old, diseased, superstitious, and reactionary Nikias, the intergeneration conflict of the Wilhelmian era as experienced by Heym finds thinly disguised expression. Gylippos, of "The Sicily Campaign," in his ugliness embodies Heym's fixed idea about his own appearance and in his ruthlessness, the quality of mind on which the youthful author occasionally prided himself (10.2.1906).

Gylippos' counterpart in "Atalanta" is Sigismondo Baffi. He too was condemned by birth to the ugliness which made his heart evil and barren until Atalanta "cured" him temporarily with her kisses. In the same period Heym wrote in his diary, with reference to his own supposed physical and moral shortcomings, that he knew love would "cure" him (3.15.1908). His private despair over the insoluble disparity between his supposed ugliness and his thirst for beauty was superimposed on the action of "The Sicily Campaign." Some of Gylippos' utterances correspond almost literally to the frequent complaints in Heym's diaries about this obsessive notion.

> Ich hass Athen, weil ich so hässlich bin,
> Weil ungerecht das Schicksal euch allein,
> Der Stadt und allen wohl, die sie bewohnen,
> Verschwendrisch Schönheit gab mit vollen Händen.
> Weil's mir den Leib zuwarf, den ich verachte,
> Und noch zum Hohn in diesen Leib einzwängte
> Dann einen Geist, der sich nach Schönheit sehnt,
> Des Sehnsucht einsam brennend sich verzehrt,
> Ein Feuer ohne Nahrung, nie erfüllt.*

> (I hate Athens, because I am so ugly,
> Because Fate gave, unjustly, only you,
> The city and all those, who live in it,
> Beauty, extravagantly and prodigiously.
> Because it allotted me the body, which I despise,
> And mockingly constrained then in this body
> A spirit, yearning for the beautiful,

Dichtungen und Schriften, II, 220. All quotations from the dramas are cited in the text by page number from this edition.

Whose yearning consumes itself in lonely flames,
A fire unnourished, never satisfied.)

These lines strikingly demonstrate how little Heym was able to objectivate and sublimate his own emotions in this phase of his artistic development. But even so, these completed plays are on the borderline of his mature literary work. From the beginning they contained elements which anticipated the characteristics of the best writing of Heym's last years. This is the reason Heym continued to occupy himself with these works even after the transition to his final phase, and in some instances he succeeded in strengthening their "mature" aspects.

These elements of maturity amount primarily to the representation of a specific world view. In the dramas the reflection of private moods and feelings began to be supplanted by the postulation of a philosophy of life. This development is, of course, concurrent with Heym's systematization of his incidental grievances and sorrows. His unfortunate experiences in the realms of love and friendship, the friction with his father, objections to his school, and so forth, all combined to convince him that mankind is the passive victim of a cruel and inexorable fate. His pessimistic fatalism determined his poetic universe. This is very directly revealed in "The Sicily Campaign," in which fate plays the decisive role. By negating all the calculations of the Greeks who failed to consider it, fate "gruesomely proved its majesty" (page 270).

Man's helpless subjugation to a tyrannical power beyond his ken or control is strikingly demonstrated in the very prominent death motif of Heym's mature work. Walter Sokel points to the connection between the personal experiences from which Heym's fatalistic outlook was derived and his literary obsession with death: "Heym's fascinated preoccupation with death, a conspicuous element in his work, can be traced partially to his early wretchedness and isolation."[1] In both "The Sicily Campaign" and "Atalanta" death not only forms the ever present background to the action, but is also invoked in its most desolate aspects by the personages.

When in the first-mentioned play the Athenian army has been routed by the Sicilians, one of the fleeing soldiers reports:

Aller Orts
Den ganzen Weg herauf, durch Baum und Wald,
Durch Berg und Sumpf und durch die Wüstenei

Verlorner Steine hängt das Totenvolk,
Mit seiner Rüstung klappernd, die geprahlt
Auf allen Strassen einst. Wie Früchte dürr,
So haben sie sich lässig aufgehängt,
Und wenn man an der Leichen Bäuche schlägt,
Dann rasseln ihre Knochen. Ach der Herbst
Hat solche Ernte hier noch nicht gebracht.
Und manche stecken fest in ihrem Sumpf,
Und in den Haaren baut das Rabenvolk
Sich Nester gross. Und wenn der Frühling kommt,
Dann trifft er viel Gerippe hierzuland,
Die schlenkernd ihn begrüssen hoch im Baum. (pages 285-86)

(Everywhere
All along the road, through trees and woods,
Through mountains and through swamps and
    through the desert
Of barren rocks the dead are hanging,
Clattering with their armor, which was once
Shown off on every street. Like dried out fruit,
They have indifferently hanged themselves,
And when you hit the bellies of the corpses
Their bones start rattling. Alas autumn
Has never yet brought such a harvest here.
And many are half swallowed by the swamps,
And in their hair the flocks of ravens build
Large nests. And when the springtime comes,
It will meet many skeletons in this land
Which greet him dangling high up in the trees.)

Another aspect of death is later presented by Gylippos:

Ich hab gehört, der Toten Leben sei
An Freude arm. Sie ziehn wie Schatten hin
In öden Wüsten und in Einsamkeit.
Sie leben ohne Erinnerung, nur ein dumpf
Und matt Gefühl von ihrer Traurigkeit
Wohnt in der leeren Brust. Sie kennen nicht
Einander und gemeinsam nicht
Beweinen sie ihr unermessnes Leid.
Sie fliehn einander stumm und kühl vorbei. (page 323)

(I have been told the existence of the dead
Lacks joy. They move around like shadows

In barren deserts and in loneliness.
They exist without memory, only a dull
And dreary feeling of their sadness lives
In their vacuous breast. They do not know
Each other and do not bewail
Together their immeasurable woe.
They flee past one another mute and cold.)

In the other play, Atalanta visualizes her death in images of even
more extreme gruesomeness than those found in Heym's poetry.

Kein Frühling ist da unten, kein Gesang.
Auf leeren Schädeln spannen graues Haar
Zum Lautenschlag des Todes Musikanten.
In eine öde Gruft bin ich gebannt.
In einen Leinensack werd ich genäht.
Und wie die Trauben in dem Herbste schwellen,
So schwell ich in des Sarges Feuchtigkeit.
Wie goldner Honig aus den Stöcken träuft,
Und in der Hitze schmilzt, so schmilzt mein Fleisch
Im Totenlaken wie gegorne Milch
Aus weissem Sacke tropft. O grauenvolles Ende.

.   .   .   .

                    Wie der Bäume Löcher
Das Harz verstopft, so klebt das Erdpech zu
Mund, Nase, Auge, Ohren. Niemand kommt,
Der es dir auskratzt. Wie ein Eiterflock,
So wächst auf deinen Augen Grind um Grind.
Die Nägel schwären an den Händen aus.
Und fallen von dem Fleisch wie Fisches Schuppen.
Der Gräber hohler Wind führt sie davon,
Gleich Blättern wirbelnd. Nimmt dir fort dein Haar,
Das wie ein Nesselwald vom Hirn dir schiesst,
Den Staub, den du aus magrer Lunge bläst. (pages 370-71)

(No springtime is down there, there is no song.
But death's musicians stretch on empty skulls
Gray hair to play upon as on a lute.
I have been banished to a barren tomb.
I have been sewn up in a linen sack.
And like the grapes swell up in autumn,
So I swell in the moisture of the coffin.
Like golden honey trickles from the combs,

And melts away in heat, so melts my flesh
Inside the shroud, like curdled milk
Drips out of a white bag. O gruesome end.

.   .   .   .

As resin clogs
The holes in trees, the pitch of earth glues up
Mouth, nose, eye, ears. Nobody comes
Who scratches it away. Like flakes of pus
It grows in layers on your eyes.
Fingernails fester from your hand.
And drop out of the flesh like fishes' scales.
Hollow sepulchral wind sweeps them away,
Twisting like leaves. It takes away your hair,
Which like a nettle forest grows upon your brain,
The dust, which issues from your meagre lungs.)

Heym's fatalistic world view has also left its mark upon the dramatis personae themselves, whose characterizations exemplify their abject subservience to the arbitrary, unknowable force which rules the universe. Interesting in this context is a letter from a publisher to whom Heym had submitted "The Sicily Campaign." This document furthermore testifies to the keen eye of the publisher's reader, who made an entirely accurate assumption about the genesis of the piece: "Your play gave us the impression that a project which goes back to a very early date had been taken up again by you and brought to a conclusion, but that the weaknesses of the first plan could not be overcome. With the sole exception of the passage of Nikias' death nothing in the piece affects us forcefully and directly; the action is always ponderously political ("es ist immer eine Haupt- und Staatsaktion") and the problem of Gylippos cannot disguise this. But what is most fatal for the play is, we think, that nothing has been made out of Alcibiades. He is in word and action such a weak figure that the deviation from history therefore seems to be particularly unmotivated" (letter 147).

The weakness for which this report criticizes the figure of Alcibiades is, of course, the very aspect of his personality which reflects Heym's views on mankind. Alcibiades' weakness symbolizes the utter passivity with which humanity submits to the fatal powers. This fatalism also appears clearly in the case of Nikias, who, like

a parody on Wallenstein, is in all his actions guided by the stars.
His death, which the publisher's reader singled out for praise,
actually shows a close affinity with Alcibiades' character as a symbolic expression of Heym's fatalism. Too weary and sick to stand
up, Nikias rolls over on his stomach on the ground and bares his
neck to the executioner who unseen steps behind him with his
sword (page 291).

The other major figure in "The Sicily Campaign," Gylippos,
at first sight seems to contradict the conception of mankind embodied in Alcibiades and Nikias. Gylippos in the course of the
action seems to control his own destiny and the destinies of the
others. The final scene makes it clear, however, that he has been
blindly driven onward by the demonic force of his jealous hate-
love for Alcibiades. When he finally has the latter in his power, he
reluctantly kills him, because he has devoted his entire life to this
purpose. But at the same time that he achieves his end, his own
existence becomes meaningless, and he sits down, caressing the
face of his victim, to wait for his own death. Thus, in the end,
all the humans are defeated by fate.

In many respects, "Atalanta" is the radical opposite of "The
Sicily Campaign." The latter has a very extensive cast, which
includes masses of soldiers and citizens; it is divided into four acts
placed respectively in Athens, Sicily, Sparta, and Asia, and covers
an unspecified, but considerable length of time. The one-act play
"Atalanta," which is less than one-quarter as long as "The Sicily
Campaign," has only three characters, is set in one room, and covers less than one hour in its action. This tendency toward general
condensation is a vast step forward compared with the prolixity of
"The Sicily Campaign" and shows Heym's greater awareness of
the nature of his talent.

But there are also points of similarity between the two works,
notably between the characters of Gylippos and Sigismondo Baffi.
Like the Spartan, Sigismondo is the active figure who seems to be
responsible for the tragic turn of events. It appears, however,
that he too is driven on by passions over which he has no control,
since they stem ultimately from the fate of having been born
ugly. And, where in the earliest versions of the text, the slander
against and murder of his stepbrother does gain Atalanta for
Sigismondo, in the subsequent changes of the conclusion he loses
his love for her, so that all has been in vain.

—Der arme Tote ist umsonst gestorben.
Ich komm dahin, dass ich ihn wecken möchte.—
Ihr seid mir gleichgültig geworden, Witwe.
Ihr seid zu wohlfeil. Meine Leidenschaft,
Die ich vielleicht einmal für Euch gefühlt,
Ist fort, zum Fenster heraus.*

(The poor deceased has died in vain.
I almost wish I could awaken him.—
I regard you with indifference, widow.
You are too easily won. My passion,
Which maybe at one time I had for you,
Has gone, out of the window.)

Herewith Sigismondo is revealed to be just as little a master of his own destiny as Gylippos. Fate has used him and his passions as an instrument for the destruction of Bartolomeo and then discarded him, depriving him of the only thing which gave his life meaning, his love for Atalanta.

The gradual development of the typical Heymian passivity and inability to determine the course of events is seen in the character of Atalanta herself. This can be traced through the original version of the play, which was called "The Wedding of Bartolomeo Ruggieri," and the three successive readings of the concluding scene of the later versions that were entitled "Atalanta."

In "The Wedding of Bartolomeo Ruggieri" Atalanta, in the end, does achieve the triumph of saving her husband from the assault by Sigismondo. She throws herself between them, sacrificing her own life and thus atoning for her misconduct. In the versions of the play entitled "Atalanta" the title figure wants to receive the fatal wound for her husband, but cannot bring herself to make the decisive move. The stage directions refer to Atalanta's mental struggle with the terrible decision and her desperate effort to sacrifice herself, which end in the admission of defeat, "No, I cannot do it" (page 392). She passively sees Bartolomeo murdered, and blames her inability to act and to give her own life for his

*Page 402. Gylippos' and Sigismondo's relations to their respective victims demonstrate the truth of a remark by Arthur Schnitzler: "Is a human being ever the fate of another? He is always only the means of which fate makes use"—"Der Ruf des Lebens," *Die Dramatischen Werke* (Frankfurt/M, 1962), I, 1024.

on the hypnotic force which Sigismondo used to subject her to his will.

> Du hast mich festgebannt mit deinem Auge,
> Du hast mich festgebunden mit der Stirn,
> Du hast mich angenagelt an den Boden,
> Du hast mich angefesselt mit dem Dolch.
> Mit unsichtbarer Schnur ward ich umschnürt.
> Ich sah den Dolch aus schwarzen Falten glänzen,
> Wie Todes offner Rachen sah's mich an.
> Da musste ich die Augen offen halten,
> Und konnte mich nicht stürzen in den Dolch.
> Ich konnt es nicht.

> (You have kept me spellbound with your eye,
> You have enchained me with your brow,
> You have pinned me down to the floor,
> You have shackled me with the dagger.
> With invisible cords I was tied up.
> I saw the dagger gleam forth from black folds,
> It looked at me like the open jaws of death.
> Then I had to keep my eyes open,
> And could not throw myself into the dagger.
> I could not.)

Sigismondo represents for Atalanta the demonic force of fate against which she is helpless. At the end of the lines quoted above she makes a gesture of "impotent" rage at him (pages 393-94). His absolute power over her mind is also expressed in "The Wedding of Bartolomeo Ruggieri." In Bartolomeo's dream his stepbrother, in the guise of a green snake, casts a spell over Atalanta, rendering her "unconscious," "will-less," and no longer in control of her body (pages 339-40).

The successive conclusions written for the "Atalanta" version of the play further demonstrate Heym's attempt to make the figure of Atalanta even more passive. In the first of the texts concerned she does actually flee with Sigismondo after the murder of Bartolomeo. According to the second reading she robs the corpse as the murderer demands, and because of this too great docility he loses interest in her and goes away by himself. The final stage direction reads, "He goes out of the door and closes it behind him. Atalanta stands up and beats wildly on the door. But the door does not yield. Thereupon she runs around the room like a savage, around and around, screams like one possessed, beats on the door again, jumps over the corpse, beats on the door again" (page 403). Although pointless, this frenzied activity of Atalanta is a form of resistance against her fate, and it is significant that Heym in the subsequent revision of this scene removed this last trace of independent willpower and reduced her to inert acceptance of her lot. "He quickly closes the secret door behind him. Atalanta half sits up by the side of the corpse and stares fixedly at the place where Sigismondo has disappeared" (page 407).

Since Heym's plays to some extent project into his creative maturity, they do open up certain literary historical perspectives. As a dramatist, Heym stood on the borderline of two periods. His choice of subject matter reveals a strong preference for classical and Renaissance themes which lend themselves to the portrayal of a unique individual.

Georg Heym's fascination with the Renaissance world is indicated by his inordinate fondness of such lesser novelistic treatments as Dmitry Sergejewitsch Mereschkowski's *Leonardo da Vinci* and Alfred Dove's *Caracosa* (7.17.1905, 5.2.1907, 10.10.1909, 12.27.1909). In this respect he has a pronounced affinity with a literary current much in evidence around the turn of the century. The widespread preoccupation at that time with the Renaissance in particular is represented by such works as Conrad Ferdinand Meyer's "Renaissance Novelle," *The Temptation of Pescara* (*Die Versuchung des Pescara*), which appeared in the year of Heym's birth, 1887; Isolde Kurz' *Florentine Novelle,* 1890; and Hugo von Hofmannsthal's *Death of Titian* (*Tod des Tizians*), 1892. Renaissance themes were particularly favored by such writers of the Neo-Romantic School as Herbert Eulenberg and Richard Beer-Hofmann.

But Heym, as a survey of his completed dramas indicates, having chosen his protagonists from history's store of great and exceptional individuals, treated them in a very unhistorical manner. He did not bring out their uniqueness, but depicted them as weak-willed victims and tools of fate—that is to say, representatives of general, amorphous humanity as he saw it. This discrepancy between his subject matter and his approach was probably the main reason why Heym's dramatic attempts, with but two exceptions, remained unfinished.

The anti-individualistic trend in Heym's creative attitude, as manifested in the dramas, links these works with the expressionistic movement which dominated the German literary scene from 1910 onward, and of which the mature Heym became one of the first great representatives.

Within expressionism passionate protests against all individuality, such as Werfel's poem "I Am Still But a Child" ("Ich bin ja noch ein Kind"), exemplify the dialectical reversal of the trend toward extreme individualism which dominated the preceding epoch. The leading motif of this poem expressed in the repeated exclamation "O Lord, disintegrate me!" shows the general expressionist preoccupation with the essence of humanity, rather than with unique personalities. "Every human is no longer an individual, tied to duty, morals, society, family. In this art form he is nothing but the noblest and most piteous: he is a human being."[2]

The subject matter of Heym's dramatic projects is thus an indication that at the stage of his artistic development which they represent, his attitude was in some respects preexpressionistic. But through his handling of these subjects, no matter how inept, he anticipated one of the main characteristics of expressionist writing.

The literary-historical position of Heym's plays can be clearly demonstrated by comparing his "Atalanta" with another specific work dealing with a Renaissance theme—Arthur Schnitzler's playlet *The Woman with the Dagger (Die Frau mit dem Dolche)*. While "Atalanta" shares setting and historical background with this work, written in 1902, the difference between the ways in which the respective authors handle similar motifs reveals the narrow limits of Heym's relationship with Neo-Romanticism and the extent of his proto-expressionist tendencies.

Each play has a cast of three characters who have comparable relations with each other. In "Atalanta" the title figure on the eve of her wedding has been seduced by Sigismondo, who had traduced her husband-to-be Bartolomeo. Schnitzler's Paola has given herself to Lionardo on the night before her husband's return from a lengthy journey. Both women deny that these transgressions give their lovers any rights over them.

Sigismondo: Vergassest
    Du, was du gestern um dieselbe Stunde
    Mir in die Hände schwurst.

    ·   ·   ·   ·   ·   ·   ·

                                  Du leugnest,
    Dass du mir folgen wolltest? (*Dicht an ihr.*)

Ist dies nicht
Der Gattin Pflicht?

Atalanta: Der Eid ist nichtig, den die Satanskunst
Mir abdrang, deiner Lügen. (page 380)

(Sigismondo: Did you forget
What yesterday at this very hour
You solemnly swore.

. . . .

You deny
You wanted to come with me? (*Close to her.*)
Is that not
Your wifely duty?

Atalanta: The oath is void, which the devilish trickery
Of your lies forced me to make.)

Lionardo: Paola, heute nacht warst du—

Paola: Die Deine!?
Versuch' es auszusprechen, da es tagt!

. . . .

Es ist nicht mehr und also war es nie!

Lionardo: Paola, nein! es war und darum ist es!
Und wird sein, und mein Recht auf dich besteht!

Paola: Ein Recht? auf mich ein Recht! Begreifst du nicht,
Dass es erlosch mit dieser Nacht Gestirnen,
Und dass du jedes Rechtes ledig bist.[3]

(Lionardo: Paola, last night you were—

Paola: Yours!?
Try to declare it, now that it is day!

. . . .

It is no more and therefore never was!

Lionardo: Paola, no! It was and therefore is!
And will be, and you still are mine by rights!

Paola: By rights? I, yours by rights! Don't you understand
Your rights have disappeared with last night's stars,
And that you have no rights at all.)

These comparable scenes indicate a vast difference in character between the two women. Atalanta's fall is the result of her emotional confusion which shows her as the helpless victim of Sigismondo's demonic plot. Paola has willfully and consciously committed an act which has left her pride and self-possession unimpaired.

The same distinction becomes apparent in a juxtaposition of two other scenes. The one from "Atalanta" looks like an inversion of that from *The Woman with the Dagger*. Schnitzler lets his Paola make a full confession as soon as her husband Remigio returns: "It is the courage of the guilty to confess their guilt!"[4] Lionardo warns her—in vain—that she may put too much trust in Remigio's magnanimity.

The tragedy in "Atalanta" hinges on the fact that Atalanta has too little faith in Bartolomeo's generosity to admit her misdeed. As Heym pointed out in a comment on the play, "In her petty feminine soul she cannot grasp that he would forgive her" (letter 155). She admits her lack of courage in the exclamation: "How can I confess it to him? Whence the courage/Whence?" (page 381). Fear is her dominating emotion, while her counterpart in Schnitzler's work indignantly rebuts her lover who thinks she is afraid: "What do you say? Fear? What, do you think I am scared?"[5]

In the final version, the concluding scene of Heym's play has a certain outward similarity with the end of *The Woman with the Dagger*. When she has stabbed Lionardo to death, "Paola remains standing motionless until the end of the scene."[6] Standing upright and holding the dagger, her immobility is expressive of the leading part she has taken in the development of the action and of her formidable strength of will and character. Atalanta, however, crouching over Bartolomeo's corpse, epitomizes the abject passivity with which Heym's creatures submit to their fate and which he wanted to illustrate with his tragedy.

Schnitzler's intentions were entirely different: he aimed to show the tenuity of the dividing line between past and present, reality and unreality, to develop the theme of the artist who exploits his family tragedies for his work, and to give an ironic comment on the female character. Pauline, in her imaginative Renaissance guise of Paola, kills her lover Lionardo, while in reality she ends by promising his modern reincarnation Leonhard another rendezvous.

Another important difference between "Atalanta" and *The Woman with the Dagger* concerns their dramatic quality. Schnitzler's characters arouse genuine interest because they are human and have their strengths and weaknesses, their good and bad points. Pauline falls far short of the level of integrity of Paola; Remigio's magnanimity contrasts sharply with his disregard for human suffering when he can use it as a subject for a painting. Lionardo, as the underdog in the action, is in some respects comparable to Atalanta. The latter begs God to send her death:

> O lösch mich aus. Ich bitte nichts als Tod.
> Ein kleines Quäntchen Tod, ein kleines Gran
> Von deinem grossen Speicher voller Tode.

> (O snuff me out. I only ask for death.
> A particle of death, a minute grain
> From your enormous silo full of death.)

And when her prayer is not granted, she asks Sigismondo to kill her:

> Liebst du mich,
> Du sagtest es, so tu mir, was ich bitte.   (page 396)

> (If you love me,
> You said you did, then do as I implore.)

Sigismondo refuses to slay her, as in Schnitzler's play Remigio ignores Lionardo's pleas to the same effect.

But whereas Atalanta resignedly accepts her fate of having to live on, Lionardo has the strength to force the solution he seeks. When his first request, "Kill me, Remigio!" is refused, he repeats it with more emphasis, "I beg you, Remigio: kill me!" Remigio rejects this demand also, whereupon:

Lionardo: I asked for death, but now I demand it!

Remigio: Your wish concerns me as little as your pleading.

Lionardo: Then I will force you to do it![7]

Lionardo's threats to make his affair with Paola public and to kill Remigio finally lead the woman to kill her lover. Thus Lionardo proves to have much more character than Atalanta, who is consistently weak, fearful, and completely passive. The other characters in Heym's play are just as little the masters of their fates, and each in his way is a mere puppet in the hands of demonic forces.

The early commentator Helmut Greulich contended that for a dramatist, Heym was not objective enough in his approach to his characters, and consequently failed to achieve the indispensable element of dramatic tension.[8] As "The Sicily Campaign" and "Atalanta" show, the origin of Heym's undramatic attitude can be traced to the fundamental composition of his personality. The archetypal motif of the serious drama is the conflict between human hybris and divine nemesis. In Heym's conception of the universe, there was no place for the former, for he saw man passively and helplessly exposed to the arbitrariness of fate.

6

Verse and Universe

WITH HIS ADMISSION to the Neue Club around the New Year of 1910, Heym's maturity as a writer may be said to have commenced. The beginning of this phase is not as sharply defined as that of the preceding one. There was no sudden involuntary change in creative attitude such as the one which in the summer of 1906 led from the early adolescent soul-searching to the extroverted display of skill and talent. On the evidence of the dramas there was a gradual transition from this intermediate state, in which momentary moods and emotions still indirectly intruded on the work, to the unified cosmology of the mature writings.

Equally gradual were the other effects of the full deployment of Heym's talent. Although naturally still interested in getting work published, he gave up the frantic attempts which marked the preceding phase: "I am not interested in propaganda any more. If my work has any value it will come to light and establish itself on its own merits" (10.5.1911). Of further significance to his change of attitude is the shift in emphasis of his creative activities from drama to poetry and, in the last year of his life, to prose. He did still, to be sure, tinker with "The Sicily Campaign" and "Atalanta" and produce a few more brief dramatic fragments, but these are qualitatively and quantitatively quite insignificant compared to his prolific creation of poems and short stories.

These works are entirely dominated by the fatalistic view of

71

mankind which Georg Heym abstracted from his lifelong, un-
availing struggle against loneliness and isolation. His mature work
is entirely devoted to the expression of the view that humanity is
in the relentless grip of fatal forces bent on terror and annihilation.
As in the dramas, so in his poetry and prose, the theme of death
is very prominent among the symbolizations and manifestations
of man's dismal lot.

In the poems three main approaches to the theme of death can
be distinguished. First, the phenomenon of death itself may be
referred to in any manner, varying from the simple mention of
the word "death" to such extensive allegorizations of a classical-
mythological nature as those found in the poem "The Land of the
Dead" ("Die Heimat der Toten").

> Die Strasse kommt der Tod, der Schifferknecht.
> Um seine gelben Pferdezähne staut
> Des weissen Bartes spärliches Geflecht.

> (Along the street comes death, the ferry-man.
> Around his yellow horse-teeth bristles
> The scanty tangle of his beard.)

Second, the state of death may be dealt with either in specula-
tions about its nature or in repeated visions of the realm of the
dead. The former can be exemplified with the following stanzas,
in which the dead in "The Morgue" ("Die Morgue") express their
hopes and fears of the future.

> Ruhen wir aus im stummen Turm, vergessen?
> Werden wir Welle einer Lethe sein?
> Oder, dass Sturm uns treibt um Winteressen,
> Wie Dohlen reitend auf dem Feuerschein?

> Werden wir Blumen sein? Werden wir Vögel werden,
> Im Stolze des Blauen, im Zorne der Meere weit?
> Werden wir wandern in den tiefen Erden,
> Maulwürfe stumm in toter Einsamkeit?

> Werden wir in den Locken der Frühe wohnen,
> Werden wir blühen im Baum und schlummern in Frucht,
> Oder Libellen blau auf den See Anemonen
> Zittern am Mittag in schweigender Wasser Bucht?

Werden wir sein, wie ein Wort von niemand gehöret?
Oder ein Rauch, der flattert im Abendraum?
Oder ein Weinen, das plötzlich Freudige störet?
Oder ein Leuchter zur Nacht? Oder ein Traum?

Oder—wird niemand kommen?
Und werden wir langsam zerfallen,
In dem Gelächter des Monds,
Der hoch über Wolken saust,
Zerbröckeln in Nichts,
—Dass ein Kind kann zerballen
Unsere Grösse dereinst
In der dürftigen Faust.

(Are we resting in a silent tower, forgotten?
Will we be waves of a Lethean river?
Or will storms drive us around wintry chimneys,
Riding like jackdaws on the fiery glow?

Will we be flowers? Will we become birds,
In the proud blue skies, in the anger of the limitless sea?
Will we be roaming in the depths of the earth,
Dumb moles in barren lonesomeness?

Will we live in the locks of daybreak,
Will we bloom in the tree and slumber in fruit,
Or blue dragonflies on the sea anemones
Tremble at noon in a bay of still water?

Will we be like a word which no one hears?
Or smoke which flutters in space at nights?
Or a crying which suddenly disturbs the happy?
Or a candle at night? Or a dream?

Or—will no one come?
And will we slowly decompose,
In the laughter of the moon,
Which rushes high over the clouds,
Crumble into nothingness,
—That a child can clutch
Our erstwhile greatness
In its poor little fist.)

The last quoted, concluding stanza stands out from the rest of the
poem because of the greater intensity of its poetic diction and

because it consists of eight short, staccato verses instead of four long ones. This suggests that the poet's answer to all the preceding rhetorical questions regarding the possibilities of reincarnation is negative, and that he is convinced that mankind faces only total, unlamented, and unremembered annihilation.

The works dealing with the realm of death can take the shape of turbulent erotic visions of the underworld of antiquity, as in the poem "Styx." More commonly, however, the land of the dead is described in terms similar to those used for the world of the living. In "Cities of the Sea" ("Die Meerstädte") the "real" cities are referred to in these lines:

> Glocken nicht brummten. Und Bettler nicht sassen am Pfad.
> Rief kein Horn, und niemand den Weg uns vertrat.
> Und die Städte alle waren wie Wände bloss.
> Sterne nur gingen über die Zinnen sehr gross.

> (Bells did not hum. No beggars sat on the road.
> No horn sounded, and no one crossed our path.
> And all the cities were like mere façades.
> Only big stars moved over the battlements.)

The "cities of the dead" are thus described in "Black Visions II" ("Schwarze Visionen II"):

> Und schwarze Fahnen wehn die langen Gassen
> Der ausgestorbnen Städte, die verstummt
> Im Fluch von weissen Himmeln und verlassen,
> Wo ewig eine stumpfe Glocke brummt.

> (And black banners wave the long alleys
> Of cities, quiet like a grave, and silent
> In the curse of white skies and deserted,
> Where eternally a dull bell hums.)

This approximation of the realms of the living and the dead has the effect of obscuring the dividing line between the two states of being. Elsewhere, too, Heym indicates that the transition from life to death is almost imperceptible.

> Wer stirbt, der setzt sich auf, sich zu erheben,
> Und eben hat er noch ein Wort gesprochen.
> Auf einmal ist er fort. Wo ist sein Leben?[1]

(He who dies sits up as if to arise,
And just now he has still spoken.
Suddenly he has gone. Where is his life?)

The passivity and utter defenselessness of the dead are in this way closely associated with the living—the visions of the realm of death are turned into symbolic interpretations of everyday reality.

The helplessness of the dead against the forces of destruction is also a crucial point in Heym's third main method of dealing with the theme of death, namely the description of the appearance of the dead, usually through an abundance of gruesome details of their decay and deformation. From the virtually limitless number of instances in Heym's poetry, the following lines from "Black Visions I" can be chosen to illustrate this thematic treatment.

> Die ersten Würmer tanzen um das fahle,
> Vom Grubenwasser bleiche Schläfenbein.
>
> Wie Ärzte stechen lang sie die Pinzette
> Der Rüssel, der im Fleische Wurzel schlägt.
> Du jagst sie nicht von deinem Totenbette,
> Du bist verflucht, zu leiden unbewegt.

> (The first worms dance around the sallow,
> Temporal bone, bleached by seepage.
>
> Like doctors they stick in the long pincers
> Of the proboscis, which takes root in the flesh.
> You cannot chase them from your deathbed,
> You are condemned to suffer motionless.)

The dead—and the living, for the distinction is slight—are defenseless against the torture inflicted on them. They cannot ward off the demonized forces which visit the blind wrath of fate upon them.

It is the lot of humanity to submit silently to its fate, for not only defense but also all protest is denied it. Human existence, symbolized by Ophelia's body floating downstream, is "mute misery."

> Im Haar ein Nest von jungen Wasserratten,
> Und die beringten Hände auf der Flut
> Wie Flossen, also treibt sie durch den Schatten
> Des grossen Urwalds, der im Wasser ruht.
>
> Die letzte Sonne, die im Dunkel irrt,
> Versenkt sich tief in ihres Hirnes Schrein.

Warum sie starb? Warum sie so allein
Im Wasser treibt, das Farn und Kraut verwirrt?

Im dichten Röhricht steht der Wind. Er scheucht
Wie eine Hand die Fledermäuse auf.
Mit dunklem Fittich, von dem Wasser feucht
Stehn sie wie Rauch im dunklen Wasserlauf,

Wie Nachtgewölk. Ein langer, weisser Aal
Schlüpft über ihre Brust. Ein Glühwurm scheint
Auf ihrer Stirn. Und eine Weide weint
Das Laub auf sie und ihre stumme Qual.[2]

(A nest of young water rats in her hair,
And the ringed hands on the river
Like fins, she floats through the shadows
Of the great forest, resting in the water.

The setting sun which errs in the darkness
Sinks deep into the casket of her brain.
Why did she die? Why does she so alone
Float in the water full of ferns and weeds?

The wind stands in the dense reeds. It shoos
The bats away like a hand.
With dark wings, moist from the water
They stand like smoke puffs in the watercourse,

Like nightclouds. A long, white eel
Slips over her breast. A glowworm shines
On her brow. And a willow weeps
Its leaves on her and her mute misery.)

The individuality of Heym's work can well be demonstrated if the above stanzas are compared with another expressionist's treatment of this traditional drowning motif. In 1912 Gottfried Benn's collection *Morgue* appeared, and it contained the following work.

Schöne Jugend

Der Mund eines Mädchens, das lange im Schilf gelegen hatte,
sah so angeknabbert aus.
Als man die Brust aufbrach, war die Speiseröhre so löcherig.
Schliesslich in einer Laube unter dem Zwerchfell
fand man ein Nest von jungen Ratten.
Ein kleines Schwesterchen lag tot.
Die andern lebten von Leber und Niere,

tranken das kalte Blut und hatten
hier eine schöne Jugend verlebt.[3]

.   .   .   .

(Beautiful Youth

The mouth of a girl, who had long lain in the reeds,
looked so chewed up.
When her breast was broken open, the gullet was full of holes.
Finally in an arbor under the diaphragm
a nest of young rats was found.
One little sister lay dead.
The others lived on liver and kidney,
drank the cold blood and had
spent a beautiful youth here.

.   .   .   .)

One major point of difference between this poem and Heym's "Ophelia" is immediately obvious. Benn calculatingly aimed at shocking by a dubious display of clinical cynicism. Heym's poem, on the other hand, is a sincere literary expression of his pessimistically fatalistic conception of the universe. The destruction and denial of the current world view in his mature work was the inevitable effect of the creative sublimation of his private fears and sorrows.

Benn's poem "Beautiful Youth" is based on ambiguity, not only in such a word as "arbor" (Laube), with its medical and everyday connotations, but also in the central line "A little sister lay dead." Ostensibly the reference is to one of the brood of rats which has made its home in the corpse. But there is possibly also an allusion to the practice of passing illegitimate daughters off as young sisters. This aspect of the verse is all the more important, since it ironically and suggestively extends the meaning of the title from the rats to the girl, and provides a motive for her suicide. Herewith, her death is marked as her own responsibility, in complete contrast to Heym's conception of death as a stage in the destruction of mankind by fate's demonic forces.

When Heym equates people with vermin, it is to stress their utter lack of will and activity.

Und die Müller sitzen tagein, tagaus
Wie Maden weiss in dem Mühlenhaus.
Und schauen oben zum Dache hinaus.[4]

(And the millers sit day in, day out
White like maggots in the mill house.
And gaze up through the roof.)

Benn associates the human fetus with the rats in a traditional
sense to express a negative opinion of the moral and ethical
qualities of mankind. His world view is just as narrowly anthropocentric as that of the average Wilhelmian German, only with a
reversed denominator.

Heym's fascination with death and decay as signs of man's
"mute misery" indicates affinity with the French symbolists. This
is confirmed not only by certain diary entries in which he praises
them (7.20.1909, 11.5.1910, 9.16.1911), but also by the evidence of
their influence on his work. This is clearest in "Ophelia" which is
an adaptation and expansion of the first section of Rimbaud's
"Ophélie." But the way in which he changed his model indicates
the narrow limits of his dependence on the Frenchman. Heym
consistently stressed his concept of death as the exemplary state
of passivity in which the human being is the defenseless prey of
forces bent on his destruction. The relevant four stanzas of Rimbaud's "Ophélie" read as follows:

Sur l'onde calme et noire où dorment les étoiles,
La blanche Ophélie flotte comme un grand lys,
Flotte très lentement, couchée en ses longs voiles.
On entend dans les bois lointains des hallalis.

Voici plus de mille ans que la triste Ophélie
Passe, fantôme blanc, sur le long fleuve noir;
Voici plus de mille ans que sa douce folie
Murmure sa romance à la brise du soir.

Le vent baise ses seins et déploie en corolle
Ses grands voiles bercés mollement par les eaux.
Les saules frissonants pleurent sur son épaule.
Sur son grand front rêveur s'inclinent les roseaux.

Les nénuphars froissés soupirent autour d'elle.
Elle éveille parfois, dans un aulne qui dort,
Quelque nid d'où s'échappe un petit frisson d'aile
Un chant mystérieux tombe des astres d'or.*

*Heselhaus, p. 172. The reflective second part and rondeau-like conclusion
of Rimbaud's poem have no counterpart in Heym's work.

(On the still, black water where the stars sleep,
White Ophelia floats like a big lily,
Floats very slowly, recumbent in her long veils.
In the distant woods hunting calls are heard.

Behold, more than a thousand years sad Ophelia
Moves, a white phantom, on the long black stream.
Behold, more than a thousand years her gentle madness
Murmurs its romance to the evening breeze.

The wind kisses her breasts and unfolds like a flower
Her great veils cradled limply by the water.
The trembling willows cry on her shoulder.
The reeds bow down on her broad dreamy forehead.

The stirred water lilies sigh around her.
Occasionally she awakens in an alder which slumbers,
Some nest from which a little quivering of wings escapes.
A mysterious song falls from the golden stars.)

Rimbaud intentionally surrounded his heroine with a sphere of
irreality. By stressing that she had already been drifting down the
river for "more than a thousand years," he turned her into a purely
legendary figure. Her reality is denied still more explicitly in the
verse where she is called a "white phantom." A more complete
contrast than Heym's conception would scarcely be possible. His
Ophelia is as tangible and real a corpse as can be imagined.
This tendency to reject Rimbaud's etherealness in favor of sub-
stantiality manifests itself even in the one line which Heym took
over almost unchanged from "Ophélie": "The trembling willows cry
on her shoulder." Heym wrote, "a willow weeps/ Its leaves on
her," and by adding the reference to the falling foliage he changed
Rimbaud's figure of speech into a concrete image.

In Heym's version nothing remains of the elusiveness, the fabu-
lous haze which envelops the images presented in the French
work. In what amounts to a parody on Rimbaud's opening lines,
Heym showed Ophelia floating down the river, not "like a big
lily," but with a nest of young water rats in her hair, "and the
ringed hands on the river/ Like fins." Especially the word "Flos-
sen" with its literal meaning of "fins" and its vulgar connotation of
"hands" is symptomatic of the difference between "Ophelia" and
"Ophélie."

Other images used by Rimbaud have also undergone characteristic changes. The water lilies have turned into ferns and weeds; the birds whose quivering wings are heard in stanza IV of Rimbaud's poem have become bats. In "Ophélie" the wind kisses the girl's breasts and unfolds her great veils like a flower upon the water. The wind in "Ophelia" has an entirely different effect—it shoos the bats away like a hand. It thus appears that Heym, apart from stressing the fact that Ophelia is a corpse, drastically departed from Rimbaud's poem in his treatment of the attitude of nature toward the human figure. Whereas the French poet instilled a compassionately gentle atmosphere into his allusions of the scenery, wind, vegetation, and animals, Heym gave his depiction of these elements an extremely sinister and threatening tone. In them he represented the demonic agents which persecute and mutilate defenseless humanity.

Unlike the French symbolists' transfigurative animation of nature, Heym's visions of nature tend toward the grotesque, as indicated by their similarity to the prints of Alfred Kubin, in which plants, trees, shrubs, implements, and buildings receive a sinister life.[5] Yet very few of Heym's poetic visions could unreservedly be classed as grotesque, not only because of the complete absence of humor,[6] but also because he alters the concept of the grotesque, which typically dissolves and disintegrates every vestige of order in the universe. "It is part of the structure of the grotesque that the categories of our world orientation break down. Since the renaissance ornamentation we have observed continuous dissolutions: the confusion of realms which are to us separate, the abolition of static elements, the loss of identity, the distortion of 'natural' proportions etc. We have encountered new dissolutions: the abolition of the thing-category, the disintegration of the historic order."[7]

Most of these criteria could, with qualification, be applied to Heym's work, but unlike the true grotesque, he goes far beyond the disintegration of the traditional world image. He postulates a new system of coordinates, which amounts to a reversal of the anthropocentric notions of the relation of man and nature. Stylistically, this leads to a peculiar reversal of the categories of animate and inanimate phenomena in his metaphors and visions. By this means mankind is consistently depicted as the soulless object of arbitary persecution by the demonic forces embodied in nature, thus manifesting man's utter defenselessness against fate.

Kurt Mautz gives the following penetrating comment on the interrelated deanimation of humanity and demonization of nature in Heym's poetry:

Like the things, the people too lose the character of reality, connection, and shape. Fragmentary like the represented object-world appears an anonymous crowd of humanity which everywhere and always belongs to it, and in this crowd the anonymous "we," both unrelated side by side and dissolved in scattered fragments of humans (voices, eyes, faces, cloaks, heads, cheeks). But whereas the things in the dissolution of their character of reality are transformed into pseudo-subjects and gain a menacing life and power of their own (the streets as barking dogs and hunting "with a gruesome sword," the "vindictive" river with "white"—that means for Heym terrible—"teeth"), so that in their lack of relation a power common to them all is manifested, through which they cooperate (the streets "hunt" the fleeing ones, the river "prevents" them from fleeing), the fragments of human being change into subjectlessness, into unrelated labile things (voices which "blow past," laughter "ran over" faces, a disembodied twosome "came past" "in yellow cloaks," heads "carried themselves off," on cheeks a red color "withers"), in thing-like remainders of impotent or distorted human nature ("trembling" voices, "sad" eyes, "blood bespattered" heads, people who flee "for fear," "malicious" voices, "yellow"—that means in Heym's color language: repulsively ugly—cloaks). In the subject character which the things, and in the object character which the people assume, the power of the things over the people is reflected, the objectivation of man in a self created world which is based on objectivation and domination of nature, on rational control over things and people. Only in their mutual relation to each other the significance of the two forms of alienation of reality is revealed: the demonizing animation of the objective and the de-animating objectivation of the living.[*]

Whereas in the first section of Heym's poem the legendary image

---

[*]Mautz, *Mythologie und Gesellschaft im Expressionismus*, p. 123. It is regrettable that Mautz couches his often relevant views in such an atrocious, nearly unreadable style—the more so since sometimes it looks as if the obscurity is intentional and aimed at letting fairly elementary observations appear as profound and mysterious revelations. But Mautz is, unfortunately, not alone in this. There seems to be an ever increasing tendency among Germanists toward this type of oracularity.

of Ophelia is used to achieve the effects described by Mautz, in the second part the title figure ceases to be the central motif. Rimbaud wrote his entire poem about an ethereal human form. Heym dealt with Ophelia in the first four stanzas and then gradually changed his point of view. From the third to the sixth stanza of Part II, Ophelia is, in fact, completely out of sight: "Invisible she swims along with the river." In this part of the poem, the cities along the river banks provide the subject matter.

The modern metropolis began to play a part in literature as soon as the Industrial Revolution had become a reality in Germany, around 1885, and in that year Julius Hart wrote such works as "On the Ride to Berlin" ("Auf der Fahrt nach Berlin") and "Berlin." The naturalist attitude was, of course, marked by a one-sided accentuation of the misery amongst the industrial proletariat, which characterized the specifically modern city.

In subsequent periods the poets' attitude to the city, be it positive or negative, was marked by an increasing tendency to treat it as an entity, rather than to single out a specific population group for attention. Instances are Dehmel's "Michel Michael," Liliencron's "A Barrel Organ Goes Past" ("Eine Drehorgel zieht vorüber"), Stefan George's "The Dead City" ("Die tote Stadt"), and Rilke in his *Book of Hours* (*Stundenbuch*).[8]

In the work of the expressionists the generalization of the city became complete, while, moreover, the hitherto implicitly or explicitly introduced idea of the country as a pendant was discarded. The absoluteness which the city thus attained in expressionist poetry reflects the demographic trend initiated by the transition from an agrarian to an industrial economy.

To the expressionists, the city, the habitat of the bourgeoisie which had created Wilhelmian Germany after its own image, became synonymous with the inhabited world as such. This explains the prominence of the city motif in the poetry of the time. Heym himself is, in fact, sometimes considered primarily as a writer of city poems. In this sense Soergel calls him a "metropolitan poet,"[9] while F. J. Schneider credits him with having expressed the modern, negative attitude to the city with more "power of formulation and persuasion" than any of his contemporaries.[10]

This does not mean that his visions of the urban scene are entirely unique or unprecedented, as demonstrated in "Ophelia" where the following lines occur:

... westlich droht
In blinde Scheiben dumpfes Abendrot,
In dem ein Kran mit Riesenarmen dräut,

Mit schwarzer Stirn, ein mächtiger Tyrann,
Ein Moloch, drum die schwarzen Knechte knien.

(westward threatens
In blind windowpanes dull red of sunset,
In which a crane gestures menacingly with giant arm,

With black brow, a mighty tyrant,
A Moloch, around whom black servants kneel.)

Victor Hadwiger in 1903 published his "La Morgue" in which the
first lines read:

In weitem Bogen schwebt der Ballen.
Durch schwere Nebel
winkt der schwarze Arm der Maschine,
es knarrt der Kran.
Verschlafene Riesen,
schaukeln die Lastenkolosse
in schwarzen Reihen
uferentlang.[11]

(In a wide arc the bale flies.
Through heavy fog
the black arm of the machine beckons,
the crane groans.
Drowsy giants,
the colossal hoists rock
in black rows
along the quay.)

The similarity between these scenes is not limited to actual
terminology and atmosphere, but extends to the essence of the
works in which they occur. Ophelia's "mute misery" has a pendant
in the fate of the dockworkers, of whom Hadwiger writes:

Kalt und stumm schleppen sie
die Pest ihres Daseins

(Cold and mute they bear
the plague of their existence)

An important difference between Heym's work and that of Hadwiger lies, however, in the possible socialist connotation of the
latter.

The same distinction exists between Heym's city poems and
those of other expressionists, many of whom in this respect from
the beginning showed traces of naturalist influence. Johannes R.
Becher's "Berlin" is an extreme case in point, with its ecstatic
visions of revolution and threats of violence.

> Wir lungern um die Staatsgebäude voll Gepränge.
> Wir halten Bomben für der Wagen Fahrt bereit.[12]
>
> (We lurk around the pompous government offices.
> We have bombs ready for the passing cars.)

Paul Zech indicated his proletarian bias even in the titles of his
early poems like "Factory Street by Day" ("Fabrikstrasse Tags")
and "Sorting-girls" ("Sortiermädchen"),[13] while Ernst Stadler in his
"Closing Time" ("Abendschluss")[14] stressed the same aspect.

Heym, neither in his private nor in his creative capacity,
evinced any interest in or sympathy with the proletariat. It would
have been incompatible with his private disdain for the masses,
and in his work humanity as a whole was so thoroughly devalu-
ated that differences between the classes lost all significance; the
demonic forces of fate did not distinguish between social strata.
When Heym did refer specifically to the underprivileged, as in
the poem "The Suburb" ("Die Vorstadt"), it happened in visions
of such apocalyptic horror and bestiality that an interpretation
in terms of class struggle is much too limited and misses the
author's point. To Heym all men were equal—equally wretched,
equally hunted and tortured by fate, equally helpless and hopeless, and all his figures, be they proletarian or legendary like
Ophelia, represent mankind in its entirety.

Like his poem "Ophelia," Heym's "The Suburb" in its approach
to the city theme shows his affinity with the French symbolists.
Here too, however, important differences reveal themselves between his attitude and that of the French poets. Baudelaire was
fascinated in a positive sense by the decaying, evil, disgusting
aspects of metropolitan life. It was to him the absolute antithesis
to nature which he detested as "a great tepid and abundant force
which penetrates everywhere."[15] Heym's attitude as expressed in

"The Suburb" is the radical opposite of this. But the poem itself shows many similarities of form and mode of expression with the works of the symbolists.

Thus, stanzas three through ten of "The Suburb" give aspects of the suburban scene which are connected only by their common dismalness. They could be placed in almost any other sequence without affecting the effectiveness of the poem as a whole. It is interesting in this connection to note Hugo Friedrich's comment on Rimbaud's "Drunken Ship" ("Bateau Ivre"): "The images are mutually incoherent. None emanates as a necessary consequence from the other, so that an arbitrariness arises which would permit the interchanging of entire stanzas."[16]

With stanza IV, Heym commenced the second, main section of "The Suburb" by presenting totally isolated parts of the human body, before focusing on the figures as a whole, which include a squatting old man with a mangy, leprous forehead. In these details there is a very marked similiarity between this poem and Rimbaud's work "The Sitters" ("Les Assis") which "speaks about a herd of animalized, degenerated, evilminded ancients. Yes, initially not even about them, but about macabre details: black tumors, pockmarks, about 'indefinable excrescences' on the front of the skull like leprous fungus on old walls."[17] Baudelaire's work also stands in close relation to the third stanza of "The Suburb," as well as to the sixth and seventh, because "Noise of omnibuses, lipless faces, old women, brass music, eyeballs saturated with bile, stale perfumes: those are some of the subjects of Rimbaud's poetically 'galvanized' modernity."[18] Stanza VIII of "The Suburb" applies the term "vagabond" to the human beings populating the suburb. In the next stanza there is mention of the creased, sleepless faces of eunuchs. Here again the parallel can be seen with the symbolists, because "when Rimbaud takes humans as the subject of a poem, they appear as indefinable strangers or caricatures."[19]

Heym dealt with the modern metropolis in a more typical, independent manner in his poem "The God of the City" ("Der Gott der Stadt").

> Auf einem Häuserblocke sitzt er breit.
> Die Winde lagern schwarz um seine Stirn.
> Er schaut voll Wut, wo fern in Einsamkeit
> Die letzten Häuser in das Land verirrn.

Vom Abend glänzt der rote Bauch dem Baal,
Die grossen Städte knien um ihn her.
Der Kirchenglocken ungeheure Zahl
Wogt auf zu ihm aus schwarzer Türme Meer.

Wie Korybanten-Tanz dröhnt die Musik
Der Millionen durch die Strassen laut.
Der Schlote Rauch, die Wolken der Fabrik
Ziehn auf zu ihm, wie Duft von Weihrauch blaut.

Das Wetter schwelt in seinen Augenbrauen.
Der dunkle Abend wird in Nacht betäubt.
Die Stürme flattern, die wie Geier schauen
Von seinem Haupthaar, das im Zorne sträubt.

Er streckt ins Dunkel seine Fleischerfaust.
Er schüttelt sie. Ein Meer von Feuer jagt
Durch eine Strasse. Und der Glutqualm braust
Und frisst sie auf, bis spät der Morgen tagt.

(He sits broadly on a block of houses.
The winds gather black around his brow.
He glares angrily, where far in solitude
The last houses lose themselves in the country.

The red belly of Baal glows in the sunset,
The great cities kneel around him.
An immense number of church bells
Surge up to him out of the sea of black steeples.

Like a Corybantian dance the music of the millions
Drones loudly through the streets.
The chimney smoke, the clouds of the factories
Waft up to him, like a bluish incense haze.

The storm smoulders in his eyebrows.
The dark evening succumbs into night.
The storms flutter, looking out like vultures
From his hair, which bristles in anger.

He stretches his butcher's fist into the darkness.
He shakes it. A sea of fire rages
Through a street. And the glowing fumes roar
And devour it, until late the morning dawns.)

The use of allegory enables Heym to employ the most graphic
terms in referring to the demonic forces which terrorize the mod-

ern industrial metropolis. The first line of "The God of the City" indicates the demon's oppressiveness in a simple but highly effective image. The rest of the stanza is indicative of his irritability and jealous anger concerning the limits of his power. It is worthy of note, however, that the possibility of living in the country—beyond Baal's reach—is not raised. It is, in fact, even precluded by the image of the last houses "losing themselves" in the country. This indicates that human habitation and life are restricted to the sphere of the city and therewith to the realm of Baal.

The next stanza expands the scene of the poem from the one city referred to in the opening quatrain to an unspecified number of "big cities." By kneeling before the demon, these cities pay homage in a manner which is indicative of religious fear. This impression is strengthened and confirmed by the vision of the innumerable church steeples pointing upwards at him. If in this stanza the atmosphere seems to be Old-Testamentarian, with Baal coming close to the idea of the awe-inspiring, wrathful God, in the next quatrain the allusion is to pagan rites and religions. The lives of the multitudes thronging the city streets are, in the only direct reference to human beings in the entire poem, characterized as a ritual for the service and glorification of the deity of the city. This is one of numerous instances in which Heym achieves a dehumanizing effect through stressing the depersonalizing collectivity of city people.

The sonnet "Berlin I" contains the line, "We saw in the narrowness/ Innumerable: streams of humans and crowding." Comparable is the description of the people's movement through the city streets in the poem "The City" ("Die Stadt"): "Innumerable humans float out and in." The loss of all individuality and the resultant degrading effect of this approach are also obvious in the reference to the "swarm/ Of the people" in "The Demons of the Cities" ("Die Dämonen de Städte"), and in the comparison of the masses of humanity with the "mire" of a swamp in the same poem. Although Heym succeeds very well in utilizing images such as these for the poetic expression of his view of mankind, in themselves these metaphors were not uncommon in the expressionist era. Becher speaks of "the mire of humans" with reference to the citizens of Berlin,[20] Wolfenstein mentions "the pulp of the masses,"[21] and Arthur Drey invokes a vision of a

Menschenmasse wie ein Meer von Raben,
Stumm fliessend, dick . . .
ein Lavastrom[22]

(Human masses like a sea of ravens,
Streaming mutely, thick . . .
a lava current)

In "The God of the City" the reference to the teeming millions serves Heym not only to reduce humanity to an anonymous, amorphous mass, but also to stress that mankind universally owes worship and homage to the god of the city. After the traditional Christian and pagan allusions, the religious aspect of the relations between the people and Baal is expressed in an image typical of the modern industrial city. The factory chimneys, like the church steeples, are directed towards him and glorify him with the "incense" of their smoke. However, all this human veneration fails to placate the deity, as indicated in the last two stanzas, which return to the viewpoint of the beginning lines of the poem. In night and storm Baal vents his wrath on the city by enveloping it in a raging fire which lasts until the end of the night.

When the city as the collective manifestation of human existence is subjected to the terror of the supernatural force allegorized by God or demons, it exemplifies the fate of mankind. With the wars and rumors of wars in the years before 1914, the depiction of the city destroyed by military force, as in "The War" ("Der Krieg"), would seem an obvious variant of this motif.

Eine grosse Stadt versank in gelbem Rauch,
Warf sich lautlos in des Abgrunds Bauch.

(A great city sank down in yellow smoke,
Threw itself without a sound into the belly of the abyss.)

Yet Heym used the war motif very sparingly. This must be due to the fact that human combat and his poetic purpose are basically irreconcilable. He wanted to express the notion that all of mankind is the helpless victim of the metaphysical forces of fate. The losers of a battle, however, are in the first instance the victims of other humans, and these, the winners, must have displayed an activity and self-assertion quite incompatible with the passivity and apathy of Heym's figures.

Heym could not overcome the discrepancy between the war motif and his creative attitude by invoking established mythological personifications of war. He did, in fact, only very seldom resort to traditional allegories of any kind.* Their familiarity would weaken the impact of his visions and deprive them of their essential quality of uniqueness.

Albert Ehrenstein did actually develop Heym's work in the direction of traditional allegorization in "The War God" ("Der Kriegsgott"), in which Ares speaks as follows:

> Heiter rieselt ein Wasser,
> Abendlich blutet das Feld,
> Aber aufreckend das wildbewachsene Tierhaupt,
> Den Menschen feind,
> Zerschmettere ich, Ares,
> Zerkrachend schwaches Kinn und Nase,
> Kirchtürme abdrehend vor Wut,
> Euere Erde.[23]

> (Gaily a stream ripples,
> In the west the field bleeds,
> But upstretching my shaggy animal head,
> Hostile to man,
> I, Ares, smash,
> Crushing weak chin and nose,
> Angrily twisting off church steeples,
> Your earth.)

Ehrenstein's desire to achieve a startling effect in spite of the worn allegorization he was using led to the exaggerated diction noticeable in these lines, and even more so in the following:

> Verstreut sind die Hoden
> Euerer Söhne
> Wie die Körner von Gurken.

> (Scattered are the testicles
> Of your sons
> Like the seeds of cucumbers.)

The consequences of the war motif are largely responsible for the difference in tone between Heym's mature work and the very

---

*His extremely free interpretation of the figure of Baal, in "The God of the City," is in this respect characteristic.

early *Marathon* cycle, plans for which go back to 1908 (8.28.1908). In this early work, the ultimately victorious Greeks are credited with the power to influence the course of history: "You bear the fortune of future generations on your spears" (sonnet VI). In the close combat scenes the victimization of one human by another is impressively depicted:

> Der stärker Perser drosselt den Hellenen.
> Dann lässt er des Erstickten Blut sich munden,
> das wie ein Bach tritt aus des Bauches Venen. (Sonnet X)

> (The stronger Persian throttles the Hellene.
> Then he drinks with gusto the blood of the choked one,
> Which runs like a river from the ventral veins.)

Introduction of mythical figures leads to an intensification of the traditional battle scenes, but does not basically change their character.

> Die Götter steigen in das Schlachtgetümmel,
> aus Griechenreihn des Phöbus Pfeile sausen,
> und Ares' Stimme füllt mit lautem Brausen
> des Meeres Tiefen, Erd und weiten Himmel. (Sonnet IX)

> (The gods descend into the battle tumult,
> Phoebus Apollo's arrows shoot forth from Greek troops,
> and Ares' voice fills with a loud roar
> the depths of sea, earth and the wide heavens.)

Only when describing the vanquished and dishonored Persians fleeing on their ships does Heym find typical images and expressions:

> Das Volk sitzt wie die Fliegen matt im Rumpf,
> An Deck, und Mast. Sie schauen vor sich hin.
> An nichts zu denken, ist ihr einzger Sinn.
> Trübsinnig, krank, verwundet, faul and stumpf. (Sonnet XIX)

> (The people sit exhausted like flies in the hull,
> On deck and mast. They gaze straight ahead.
> Their only wish is to think of nothing.
> Melancholy, ill, wounded, apathetic and dull.)

To maintain the tone of these lines throughout an entire poem is, in view of the motif, a poetic *tour de force*, which Heym has not often attempted, and only once quite successfully executed. "The War," the poem in question, is therefore not representative of a large number of similar works. But by forcing the poet to overcome the difficulties inherent in the subject matter, this poem is revealing in that Heym's characteristic world view and style are very clearly reflected in it. For this reason it merits more extensive consideration.

The resistance of the subject matter to Heym's concept of the universe appears to have resulted in a closer approximation of the grotesque style than is to be found elsewhere in his *oeuvre*. Usually he went beyond the grotesque destruction of the traditional world image, and postulated a new, negative coordinate system. In "The War," however, the fundamentally interhuman nature of the war motif prevented its complete integration into the polarity of cruel metaphysical force and tortured humanity which determined Heym's poetic universe. The furthest he could go in that direction—without evoking a traditional, familiar Ares-like figure—was the disintegration of all cosmic order. This normally was only an intermediate step toward the postulation of his own world view, but it was the very aim and goal of the grotesque. On the level of poetic expression, the unusually grotesque character of "The War" manifests itself in the lack of concreteness of the war personification.

Heym's demons and gods are generally credited with sufficient visual features to make them assume a more or less fixed appearance. The god of the city in the poem of that name has a brow, a belly, eyebrows, hair, and a butcher's fist. Feet, a chin, knees, hands, a neck, horns, and hooves are attributed to the demons in "The Demons of the Cities." If fate is not embodied in such allegoric figures, Heym does let its destructive force take shape in aspects of nature, as, for instance, in "Ophelia."

In contrast to such substantial images, the protagonist of "The War" is almost exclusively referred to by the abstract pronouns "he" and "it." Heym's only concessions to his urge toward concrete expressions are the references to a hand and a head in the verses: "And he crushes the moon in his black hand" and "And it resounds when he swings his black head." Heym's highly developed visual imagination apparently could not be completely restrained and, in a poem conceived around an undefined central figure, asserted itself in these small concrete personifying traits.

A similar intrusion of the optic phantasy can be observed in one
of the other rare instances where Heym introduced an unidentified
phenomenon:

> Etwas will über die Brücken,
> Es scharret mit Hufen krumm[24]

> (Something wants to get over the bridges,
> It paws with crooked hoofs)

In "The War" the far-reaching if not complete intangibility of
the central concept is accentuated through the use of the adjective
"unrecognized" in the first stanza, and reaches a climax in the
following lines:

> In den Gassen fasst es ihre Schulter leicht.
> Eine Frage. Keine Antwort. Ein Gesicht erbleicht.
> In der Ferne wimmert ein Geläute dünn,
> Und die Bärte zittern um ihr spitzes Kinn.*

> (In the alleys it lightly grasps their shoulders.
> A question. No answer. A face turns pale.
> In the distance a thin chime wails,
> And their beards tremble on their pointed chins.)

This scene is characteristically grotesque in Wolfgang Kayser's
meaning of the term. After the provisional postulate that "the
grotesque is the alienated world,"[25] Kayser continues: "But who is
it that effects the alienation of the world, who announces himself
in menacing inscrutability: we reach only now the last depth of
horror at the transformed world. Because these questions remain
without an answer. . . . As soon as we could name the powers and
assign them a place in the cosmic order, the essence of the grotesque would be affected. . . . What approaches remains incomprehensible, inexplicable, impersonal. We could use a new formulation: *the grotesque is the stylization of the 'It,'* that 'ghostly' It
which Ammann has defined as the third meaning of the impersonal pronoun (beside the psychological one—it pleases me—and
the cosmic one—it rains, it thunders)."[26] Only in the concluding

---

*In the last verse the tone is strikingly similar to the opening line of Jakob
van Hoddis' famous poem "End of the World" ("Weltende"): "The bourgeois'
hat flies from his pointed skull" ("Dem Bürger fliegt vom spitzen Kopf der
Hut").

line of "The War" does Heym, through an Old-Testamentarian allusion to God, succeed in synthesizing the untypically grotesque
treatment of the war which is forced upon him by the nature of
this motif with the polarity of his own world image: "Brimstone
and fire rain down upon Gomorrah."[27]

In a sense, if this poem is regarded by itself and without
reference to Heym's *oeuvre* as a whole, Johannes Pfeiffer is justified in saying: "The image of Gomorrah offered as a crowning
seal of the whole poem makes a far-fetched impression . . . the
more so because nowhere before are essential traits discernible
which point ahead to the symbol of Sodom and Gomorrah or even
lead up to it with absolute necessity."[28] The Biblical allusion can
only be appreciated in the larger context of Heym's poetic cosmos
with its polarity of metaphysical fate and earthbound, spiritless
humanity. The lack of integration between the last verse and the
rest of the poem, which Pfeiffer, from his viewpoint, correctly
criticizes, is further evidence of the discrepancy between the war
motif and Heym's creative approach. Without analyzing the relationship between "The War" and the poet's conception of the
universe, Pfeiffer obviously sensed this tension when, on the basis
of stylistic arguments, he denied that the poem as a whole had
artistic merit. Although the basis of his judgment is somewhat
narrow, his interpretation is more perceptive and valuable than
is Friedrich Leiner's critique, which can only be called superficial
and futile[29] in the light of such statements as: "Observe the sharp
ü, äu and i. . . ." Leiner's comment on the concluding verse of
"The War" is also characteristically trite. That Heym designates
the war-destroyed city as a Gomorrah "illuminates in a flash his
attitude toward the whole modern world. In his opinion it is ripe
for destruction."

If war, as the instrument of fate, in this poem undergoes an
atypical and somewhat problematical treatment, the representation
of humanity conforms to Heym's customary style. The shadow
thrown ahead by the approaching catastrophe casts a spell over
the people, halting their movements and arousing fear and un-
certainty in them.

> In den Abendlärm der Städte fällt es weit,
> Frost und Schatten einer fremden Dunkelheit,
> Und der Märkte runder Wirbel stockt zu Eis.
> Es wird still. Sie sehn sich um. Und keiner weiss.

(In the evening noise of cities everywhere,
Frost and shadows of a strange darkness fall,
And the whirlpool of the markets turns to ice.
Silence descends. They look around. And no one knows.)

The human inability to know and comprehend, let alone control,
the forces which erupt in the world is emphasized in the im-
perious attitude of the war demon.

Auf den Bergen hebt er schon zu tanzen an
Und er schreit: Ihr Krieger alle, auf und an!

(On the mountains he commences to dance,
And he shouts: All you warriors, to arms!)

War presses mankind into its service; it is not an interhuman but
a superhuman phenomenon. Man's only function in the cataclysm
is to be passively sacrificed and destroyed. He is even denied the
dignity of an individual death.[30] Humanity suffers and dies in
collectivity and anonymity. "Innumerable corpses" lie stretched
out, covered by the white birds of death. Avoiding all direct
reference to humanity, Heym describes man's gruesome fate in a
derogatory image suggestive of insects or vermin.

Und was unten auf den Strassen wimmelt hin und her,
Stösst er in die Feuerhaufen, dass die Flamme brenne mehr.

(And that which on the streets down there swarms to and fro,
He sweeps into the mass of flames to make the fire burn
    more fiercely.)

These lines are also characteristic of the prominent part which
fire plays in the destruction of the human world. Many verses are
devoted to a description of the holocaust produced by war.

In die Nacht er jagt das Feuer querfeldein
Einen roten Hund mit wilder Mäuler Schrein.
Aus dem Dunkel springt der Nächte schwarze Welt,
Von Vulkanen furchtbar ist ihr Rand erhellt.

Und mit tausend roten Zipfelmützen weit
Sind die finstren Ebnen flackend überstreut

.   .   .   .

Und die Flammen fressen brennend Wald um Wald,
Gelbe Fledermäuse zackig in das Laub gekrallt

(In the night he drives the fire across the fields,
A red dog howling from wildly gaping jaws.
Out of the darkness comes the black world of nights,
Its rim terribly illuminated by volcanoes.

And with a thousand red nightcaps
All dark plains are flaring up everywhere

. . . .

And the flames devour burning forest after forest,
Yellow bats jaggedly clawing at the leaves)

The unusual abundance, even for Heym, of metaphoric variations
of the fire motif compensates for the scarcity of visual features
which could be connected with the phenomenon of war without
coming too close to the mythological war gods.

At the same time, the fire motif links "The War"—and the
numerous other works by Heym in which it occurs—with other
world-destruction poetry based on ancient Biblical traditions, such
as the "Muspilli":

so inprinnant die perga . . . suilizot lougiu der himil
. . . prinnit mittilagart . . . daz preita uuasal allaz
uarprinnit[31]

(then the mountains burn . . . the sky smolders with fire
. . . the world burns . . . the wide marshes are entirely
burnt)

The fires with which war ravages the human world are all the
more terrifying and spectacular because of the night setting of
"The War." This combination of fire and darkness is almost a
stereotype in those poems of Heym which portray the annihilation
of mankind. "The Demons of the Cities" opens with these lines:

Sie wandern durch die Nacht der Städte hin,
Die schwarz sich ducken unter ihrem Fuss.

(They wander through the night of the cities
which stoop down darkly under their foot.)

The concluding verses of this work read:

Erdbeben donnert durch der Städte Schoss
Um ihren Huf, den Feuer überloht.

(Earthquakes thunder through the laps of the cities
Around their hoofs, over which fire blazes.)

Among other examples, the following stanzas from "Black Visions II" are particularly illustrative of the striking visual contrasts
which the juxtaposition of night and flames yields.

Der grossen Städte nächtliche Emporen
Stehn rings am Rand, wie gelbe Brände weit.
Und mit der Fackel scheucht aus ihren Toren
Der Tod die Toten in die Dunkelheit.

.   .   .   .

Die schwarzen Brücken werfen ungeheuer
Die Abendschatten auf den dunklen Strom.
Und riesiger Lagunen rotes Feuer
Verbrennt die Luft mit purpurnem Arom.[32]

(The nocturnal galleries of the big cities
Stand around the edge, large like yellow conflagrations.
And with its torch death chases the dead
Out of their gates into the darkness.

.   .   .   .

The black bridges throw immensely
The evening shadows on the dark stream.
And the red fire of enormous lagoons
Burns the air with a purple aroma.)

Night is more, however, than merely an effective backdrop for
the holocaust of world destruction. There is a much closer connection between the two, as is indicated by the concluding stanza
of "The God of the City." The demonic protagonist of the poem
"stretches his butcher's fist into the darkness" and a sea of fire
engulfs the city and consumes it *until* "late the morning dawns."
In other words, only during the night are cities and humanity
threatened with destruction by fire. The coincidence of darkness
and flames in many poems is determined by the mutual relationship which, in Heym's usage, exists between these motifs. Night
is, in effect, a *conditio sine qua non* for the outbreak of the conflagrations, as is confirmed by the fact that many poems contain
night scenes without fire, whereas the latter only occurs in con-

junction with darkness. Night thus appears to be the source of the destructive energy embodied in the blaze—and, on the evidence of other poems, of many other demonic powers which menace human existence.

This function of darkness as the ominous element from which spring the forces of a cruel fate bent on annihilation and terror is nowhere more clearly expressed than in the following verses from the poem "Why do you, white butterflies, so often come to me?" ("Was kommt ihr, weisse Falter, sooft zu mir?"):

> Was ist das Leben? Eine kurze Fackel
> Umgrinst von Fratzen aus dem schwarzen Dunkel
> Und manche kommen schon und strecken
> Die magren Hände nach der Flamme.

> (What is life? A brief torch light
> Around which grimacing faces leer out of the darkness,
> And many hurry by and stretch
> Their thin hands toward the flame.)

Elsewhere mention is made of the

> . . . schwere Nacht, die auf den Schläfern liegt
> Und ihre Stirn mit Qualen weiss bereift.[33]

> (. . . heavy night, which lies upon the sleeping people
> And covers their brows with a white hoarfrost of sorrows.)

Again and again it is the night "which brings disaster,"[34] filled with mysterious, ominous signs from which, blindly groping, the people flee—in vain, as the first gray light of dawn reveals.

> Doch manche müssen einsam weit noch gehen
> Um sich in dunkle Nächte zu verbergen
> Wo schwer im Himmel sich die Wolken winden.

> Sie hören oft ein grosses Wagenrollen
> Und schattenhafte Pferde schnell verschwinden
> In Strassen fort und Mauern dunkelvollen.

> Und manchmal sehen sie in hohen Stürmen
> Den grauen Mond in Falten und verquollen
> Und Nachtgevögel singet in den Türmen.

> Im Irrsal suchen sie den Weg in Fernen
> Und tasten mit den Händen rund, den blinden,

Und hinter ihnen kichern die Laternen,
Die schnell in trübe Nacht hinab entschwinden.

Doch in der Dächer Sturz und Häuser Engen,
In leerer Giebel ausgebrannten Sparren,
Sind viele Tote, die im Kühlen hängen
Und mit dem Fuss das Morgengrauen scharren.[35]

(But many still have far to go alone
To hide themselves in dark nights
Where the clouds twist heavily in the sky.

Often they hear a great rolling of wagons
And shadowy horses disappear rapidly
Away into streets and walls, full of darkness.

And often they see in high storms
The gray moon creased and bloated
And nightbirds, singing in the towers.

In the confusion they try to find the way
And grope around with their blind hands,
And behind them chuckle the lanterns,
Which rapidly move away in the gloomy nights.

But in the fall of roofs and the narrowness of houses,
In the burnt out beams of empty gables
Are many dead, who hang in the coolness
And scrape with their feet the gray light of dawn.)

Several of the motifs in these verses recur in other poems, as can
be seen in both the birds of the night which turn "like shadows
and evil thoughts"[36] and, especially, the moon.

In a logical extension of the night motif, Heym frequently
embodied the demonic forces emanating from the night in the
guise of the moon. An extreme instance occurs in the poem
about "The Sleeping People" ("Die Schläfer"):

                    die bewacht
    Der kalte Mond, der seine Gifte träuft
    Wie ein erfahrner Arzt tief in ihr Blut.

                    (who are guarded
    by the cold moon, who lets his poison drip
    like an experienced doctor deep into their blood.)

Such treatment of the moon motif makes it obvious that Heym's idea of night as the source of the forces with which fate persecutes mankind has taken him far away from the traditions of German poetry, according to which, in the words of Eichendorff, the "silent night" was regarded as the "comfort of the world." Of Heym's contemporaries, Georg Trakl echoed this traditional sentiment in the verse, "Beautiful is the silence of the night."[37] With specific reference to the moon, the Claudius-Goethe-Eichendorff line was also continued in the expressionist era. René Schickele wrote, "Vessel of faith, you moon in the clear sky";[38] Else Lasker Schüler, "O I am so sad—the face in the moon knows it";[39] Kurt Heynicke, "O let us smile above the valleys of mankind—/ like the soul of the silver moon,/ which dreams";[40] and Walter Hasenclever, "Moon./ Gazelles call."[41]

However, Heym was by no means the first or only nonconformist in this respect. Nietzsche called the moon "evil" and "unreasonable";[42] and Theodor Däubler, in a satirical poem entitled "The Mute Friend" ("Der stumme Freund"), wrote, "The moon disseminates the pale seeds of death."[43] From Alfred Lichtenstein stem the lines, "at the side gleaming high and far away lurks/ The poisonous moon, that fat mist spider."[44] The last image is very reminiscent of the "spider arm" with which Heym once attributed the moon.[45] Such animations of the motif are a natural consequence of the urge to visualize the demonic power with which the moon has been invested. In other poems Heym's tendency to give concrete expression to the emotional value of the moon leads to an adaptation of the "man in the moon" tradition. Instead of the benevolent features that the moon has in children's books, in Heym's visions it has a rather ominous, sinister appearance, as befits the personification of a malevolent fatal force: "An enormous skull, white and dead,"[46] "the moon . . . with its big white head,"[47] "And gigantic moons/ Rose over the roofs on stiff legs."[48] In the first stanza of "Half Sleep" ("Halber Schlaf") the personification is less fragmentary.

> Und der Mond wie ein Greis
> Watschelt oben herum
> Mit dem höckrigen Rücken.

> (And like an old man the moon
> Waddles around up there
> With his hunched back.)

Heym's treatment of the moon motif appears to be determined by his consistent trend towards concrete imagery, and by his conception of the night as a time of terror and persecution for mankind. Kurt Mautz' endeavor to interpret the moon in Heym's *oeuvre* as a projection of his father imago does not only seem rather strained, but actually obscures the real significance of the motif in his visions of night.[49] In his generally perceptive study Mautz ignored the basic fact that Heym in his mature poetry completely sublimated his private experiences and emotions in symbols of universal validity.

In Heym's arsenal of poetic motifs the moon really plays the part of one of the embodiments of fate's demonic forces which persecute and terrorize humanity especially relentlessly at night. This is established by direct reference to such texts as "The Lunatics" ("Die Irren") and "The Fever Hospital" ("Das Fieberspital"). As their titles indicate these poems deal with creatures who in their physical and mental deterioration symbolize the general dehumanization of man, which state, in turn, characterizes Heym's poetic universe. The normal dismal condition of these fever patients and lunatics, which is depicted in the introductory stanzas, worsens with the advent of night as out of the gathering darkness their demonic tormentors assail them in force. In both poems the terrors to which the people are subjected are presented as hallucinations, and in "The Lunatics" the hallucinated state which overcomes them at sunset is introduced by the moon motif: "Evening enters on red soles" and the lunatics "softly singing fall asleep." Then, at the same time as "out of the ethereal sea dreams as big as suns move through their blood on red wings," the moon appears.

> Auf ihrem Schlummer kreist der blaue Mond,
> Der langsam durch die stillen Säle fliegt.

> (Over their slumber circles the blue moon,
> Which flies slowly through the silent wards.)

The climax of the succession of horrors which hereupon reduces the sufferers to abject panic is the appearance of death, which "shows its white corpse's skin" and forces an entrance to claim his victims.

In "The Fever Hospital" other agents of fate assume human guise.

Auf ihrem Dache sitzt ein Mann im Stuhl
Und droht den Kranken mit dem Eisenstab.

(On their roof a man sits in the rafters
And threatens the sick with his iron bar.)

In "The Lunatics" the tormentors are referred to as ghosts, which only through their physical maltreatment of the lunatics gain concreteness.

Gespenster sitzen um sie her und knüllen
Den Hals wie Stroh. Ihr weisser Atem zischt.

(Ghosts sit around them and crumple
Their necks like straw. Their white breath hisses.)

In the concluding verses of the relevant section of this poem the bird motif is introduced. This motif repeatedly serves in Heym's poetry to visualize the forces with which fate, predominantly at night, persecutes humanity.

Ihr Haar wird bleich, und feucht vor kaltem Grauen.
Sie fühlen Hammerschlag in ihrer Stirn,
Und grosse Nägel spitz in Geierklauen,
Die langsam treiben tief in ihr Gehirn.

(Their hair turns pale and moist from cold horror.
They feel a hammer strike their brows,
And large, sharp nails held in vulture's claws,
Which slowly penetrate deeply into their brain.)

Significant, as an indication of the ominous atmosphere which usually surrounds birds in Heym's poetry, is his preference for vultures, ravens, crows, and the like. In the short poem "April," two large crows flutter excitedly to a brown thorn bush in the green gully. This dreary landscape thus derives a touch of suspense which makes the entire scenery seem provisional and insecure.

In "And the Horns of Summer Fell Silent" ("Und die Hörner des Sommers verstummten") the desolation of the deserted, perishing countryside and cities is emphasized by the final stanza in which the ravens, erring like sombre thoughts, express a mood of utter despair and a sense of futility.

Und es sank der Schatten der Nacht. Nur die Raben noch irrten
Unter den drückenden Wolken im Regen hin,

Einsam im Wind, wie im Dunkel der Schläfen
Schwarze Gedanken in trostloser Stunde fliehn.[50]

(And the shadow of night sank. Only the ravens still roamed
Around in the rain under heavy clouds,
Alone in the wind, as in the darkness of the skull
Dark thoughts wheel in a disconsolate hour.)

To complete the description of the barren, icebound world given
in the first three stanzas of "The Wanderers" ("Die Wanderer")
as the background for the procession of dead souls, the poet
introduces "The ravens which swim in the gray heights." When
a black storm extinguishes the "apprehensive light" of a sombre
evening in the poem "Arabesque" ("Arabeske"), the atmosphere
created by this accumulation of gloomy words is reinforced by the
following verse:

Aus abgestorbnen Eichen jagt und stürmt
Ein Rabenvolk, wie schwarzer Schneefall dicht.

(Out of dead oaks drives and storms
A flock of ravens, dense like a black snowstorm.)

These birds also play a part in the advent of the "great death"
which envelops the earth in the poem "But Suddenly There Is
Much Death I" ("Auf einmal aber kommt ein grosses Sterben I").

Die Raben steigen in die Abendröte.
Und plötzlich dorret trocken das Geäste.*

(The ravens rise into the red of sunset.
And suddenly the branches wither.)

At midnight when the mice and spiders dominate the market
places in "The Markets" ("Die Märkte") the unhappiness is increased by the ravens which throw dung. The use of ravens and
crows to indicate forlornness and despair reaches a climax in the
fourth stanza of the poem "With the Traveling Ships" ("Mit den
fahrenden Schiffen"). In a parody of the tale of Noah, all that
these birds carry with them are symbols of death and barrenness.

Raben und Krähen
Habe ich ausgesandt,
Und sie stoben im Grauen

*In Dichtungen und Schriften, I, the verb in the last line is given as "dar-
ret," but this is most likely a misprint.

Über das ziehende Land.
Aber sie fielen wie Steine
Zur Nacht mit traurigem Laut
Und hielten im eisernen Schnabel
Die Kränze von Stroh und Kraut.

(Ravens and crows
I have sent out,
And they rushed in the gray light
Over the swirling land.
But they fell like stones
At night with a sad sound
And held in their iron beaks
The wreaths of straw and weeds.)

There appears to be a close link between the bird and the star motifs in Heym's works. Frequently the two merge, as for example in the concluding lines of "Arabesque."

Und vor dem Sturm einher am Himmelsraum
Entfliegt mit schnellem Flug der Abendstern.

(And ahead of the storm there flies in the sky
With rapid flight the evening star.)

A star is also "ornithized" in the vision of the "celestial expanse" where a pale star "beats its wings."[51] To this group of images further belong Saturn, whose "yellow hairy wing flew/ Through the forest's entanglement,"[52] and the golden feathers which the comets in the poem "The Deaf Ones" ("Die Tauben") spread out in the night. It is consistent with the interrelation between these motifs that the stars themselves also frequently play the part of threatening signs of approaching doom. The close of "The Suburb" which envisions the "green bell of heaven/ where soundlessly the meteors move far," is very similar to the concluding stanza of "The Flying Dutchman" ("Der fliegende Holländer").

Masslose Traurigkeit. In Nacht allein
Verirrt der Wandrer durch den hohen Flur,
Wo oben in der dunklen Wölbung Stein
Gestirne fliehn in magischer Figur.

(Immeasurable sadness. Alone in the night
The wanderer roams through the fields on high,

Where in the stone of the dark dome
Stars flee in magic constellations.)

A much more ominous tone prevails when the star and fire
motifs are combined to indicate the evil, destructive powers invested in the night.

Auf Schlangenhälsen die feurigen Sterne
Hängen herunter auf schwankende Türme,
Die Dächer gegeisselt. Und Feuer springet,
Wie ein Gespenst durch die Gasse der Stürme.[53]

(On snakes' necks the fiery stars
Hang down on swaying towers,
The roofs are whipped. And fire jumps
Like a ghost through the alleys of the storms.)

Similar in atmosphere, but somewhat more extensive, is the opening vision of "The people stand leaning forward in the streets,"
in which the humans are portrayed as they observe and attempt
to exorcise

. . . die grossen Himmelszeichen,
Wo die Kometen mit den Feuernasen
Um die gezackten Türme drohend schleichen.

(. . . the great cosmic signs
Where the comets with the fiery noses
Menacingly prowl around the battlements of the towers.)

The poem originally appeared in the collection *Umbra Vitae;* this
title immediately associates the concept of darkness with that of
life, thus suggesting that the persecution and torture to which
man is exposed particularly and intensively during the night
constitutes the very essence of human existence.

7

Prose of Pessimism

IN THE LAST YEARS of his life Georg Heym, apart from the poetry
on which his reputation is based, also wrote a number of prose
works. A small collection of these was published posthumously
in 1913 under the title *The Thief: A Novelle Book (Der Dieb:
Ein Novellenbuch).* Heym himself prepared these stories for
publication in the last days before his death. In a letter to his
publisher Ernst Rowohlt, written on January 12, 1912, he announced: "The novelle will be sent to you next Monday or Tuesday" (letter 153). But on Tuesday, January 16, 1912, Heym was
dead.

The collection consists exclusively of works written during the
last year of his life, as is evident from his correspondence with his
publisher. In his first letter to Rowohlt, written on December 4,
1910, he described his prose works written before that date as
dealing "practically exclusively with the erotic problem" (letter
27). It is obvious that none of these early efforts were included

*Published in Leipzig. For a more detailed discussion of Heym's prose, see
my articles: "Sources and Subject Matter in Two Short Stories by Georg
Heym," *AUMLA. Journal of the Australasian Universities Language and
Literature Association,* No. 12 (November, 1959), 52-57; "Georg Heyms Prosasammlung *Der Dieb*—ein Novellenbuch?" *Levende Talen,* No. 215 (June, 1962),
352-62. The latter deals primarily with the structure of the stories and with
their relation to Heym's outlook on humanity.

in *The Thief*. Heym was well aware that they were unsuitable for publication. In the letter just cited, he stated this specifically. In a postscript to his second letter to Rowohlt, written only two days later, he wrote, "I have actually planned a few novelle. But for lack of time I cannot execute them for the time being. In the middle of January I will get to work on them" (letter 28). It thus appears that immediately after his first contact with Rowohlt, who had written to Heym on November 30, 1910, requesting a manuscript for publication "be it lyric poetry or prose" (letter 25), Heym decided to utilize this opportunity to the fullest extent by composing some suitable prose works in addition to his poetry.

In accordance with this plan, during 1911 he produced a number of stories, and as each one reached completion, he submitted it to Rowohlt. But whereas his earlier works had been unsuitable because of their erotic themes, Rowohlt now raised objection to the extreme morbidity of the new stories, saying that he had severe misgivings about publishing them. He added, "Much as I personally like the stories, yet I am firmly convinced that it will be completely impossible to find even a very small reading and buying public for a book which deals exclusively with mad feverish diseased people, cripples and corpses" (letter 125).

Rowohlt's criticism elicited a hostile reaction from Heym, who threatened to look for another publisher for his book. He defended his case with the reminder that Octave Mirbeau's book *Garden of Tortures* (which he referred to under the German title *Der Garten der Qualen*), "which deals only with physical tortures," was in its twentieth edition. Further he observed: "What I would as yet write in the way of novelle would in any case all be on this level. Moreover I am now going in a different direction. The direction of the novella is not mine at all . . ." (letter 127).

Although, as Rowohlt observed, Heym's prose is on the whole rather limited in the range of its subject matter, and on Heym's own evidence represents only a passing phase in his development as an author, the stories in *The Thief* are not without literary merit. They are, moreover, in form and content highly indicative of Heym's world view. In both respects, the work entitled "The Fifth of October" ("Der fünfte Oktober"), which opened the original collection, is the most important of the seven stories concerned.

THE FIFTH OF OCTOBER

The Municipal Council of Paris had posted huge bills all over the city, announcing that a convoy of breadcarts was due to arrive from Provence on the fifth of October. On that day crowds of emaciated Parisians roamed the streets, awaiting their deliverance from starvation, dreaming of paradises of plenty.

They crowded in front of the locked-up cellars of the bakeries and peered down on the empty baking troughs, which stood behind the barred windows. They gazed into the black mouths of the gigantic ovens which, like them, were hungering after bread.

In a street on Mont Parnasse a bakery was broken into, more out of boredom, to pass the time of day, than in the hope of finding any bread on the shelves.

Three men, coal-carriers from St. Antoine, dragged the baker out of his house. They threw down his white wig and stood him under the lantern over his door. One of them took off his belt, made a noose out of it and threw it around the baker's neck. Then he held his black fist under his face and shouted at him: "You goddam weevil, now we're going to hang you."

The baker began to wail, and looked for assistance among the onlookers. But he found only grinning faces.

The cobbler Jacob stepped to the front and said to the rabble: "Gentlemen, we'll let the swine go, but first he must repeat a prayer after me."

"Yes, repeat a prayer," whimpered the baker. "Let me repeat a prayer."

Jacob started: "I am the goddamned skunk-baker."

The baker repeated. "I am the goddamned skunk-baker."

Jacob: "I am the black dough-Jew, I stink at a thousand yards."

The baker: "I am the black dough-Jew, I stink at a thousand yards."

Jacob: "Every day I pray to the fourteen holy saints, that no one may find out, what I put into the bread."

The baker repeated that, too.

The public chuckled. An old woman sat down on the steps and cackled with laughter, like an old hen laying an egg.

Jacob himself could not carry on for laughing.

This funny performance went on a while longer, till finally

the people got bored by it. They left their victim standing with his noose around his neck.

It started raining heavily, the people ran for cover. The baker had disappeared. Only his white wig was still lying in the middle of the square, it began to dissolve in the water. A dog took it in its jaws and dragged it away.

Gradually the rain subsided, and the people came out into the streets again. Hunger started gnawing anew. A child had a fit of cramps, the bystanders looked on and gave good advice.

Suddenly the rumor went round: "The breadcarts are coming! The breadcarts are coming!" And everyone started pushing out through the city gates. They came in the countryside, into the barren fields, they saw the empty sky and the long row of poplars alongside the road, which in the distance merged with the flat horizon of the plains. Overhead, a flight of ravens flew toward the city.

The streams of people poured into the fields. Many had empty bags on their shoulders, others baskets, pots, to carry the bread away in.

And they waited for the carts, searching the rim of the sky like a tribe of astronomers, looking for a new star.

They lingered and lingered, but they saw nothing except the clouds and the storm, which bent the tall trees this way and that.

From a church steeple the strokes of noon sank slowly down. A terrible weariness came over the motionless masses, apathy fell paralysing like a thick blanket over their white faces.

Oh, they had no will left. Hunger slowly throttled them, and a martyrdom of terrifying dreams unmanned them in their sleep.

Around the edge of France, huge trestle tables stood swaying under a load of enormous dishes. The people wanted to go toward them. But they were tied down on big racks, and the terrible opium of hunger had numbed their blood and frozen it into black cinders. They wanted to scream: "Bread, bread, only a mouthful, mercy, have pity, only a mouthful, dear God." But they could not open their lips, terrible, they were struck dumb. How terrible, they could not move at all, they were paralysed.

And black dreams fluttered over the groups, which stood and lay abjectly together, condemned to eternal death, stricken with eternal dumbness, doomed to submerge again in the belly of Paris, to suffer, to hunger, to be born and to die in an ocean of black darkness, of public jails, of hunger and slavery, squeezed out by bloodthirsty tax-lessees, emaciated, wasted, wilting like old parchment in the biting air of their squalid dens, doomed, finally to die in the filth of their beds and with their last breath to curse the priest, who had come in the name of his God, in the name of the State and of Authority, to wring their last pennies from them as a gift to the Church.

The sun never shone in their slums. They scarcely knew what it looked like. Now and again they saw it for an hour or two in the afternoon, as it floated over the city, enveloped in a murky haze. And then it disappeared. Like black polyps the shadows came out from under the houses again and crawled up their walls.

How often these people had gazed at the wide sunny lawns of the Garden of the Grenadiers. They had gawked at the dances of the ladies of the court, the gilded crooks with which the cavaliers played at being shepherds, the obeisances of the Moors, the trays full of oranges, biscuits, confectionery, the golden coach in which the Queen drove slowly through the park like a Syrian goddess, an incredible Astarte, stiff with white silk and glistening like a saint with a thousand pearls.

Oh, how often had they drunk from the fragrance, the flavor of the musk, how often had they almost been suffocated by the delicious perfume of amber, which wafted out of the Park of Luxembourg as out of a mysterious temple. Oh, why weren't they allowed in just once, to sit on a velvet chair like that just once, just once to ride in a coach like that. They would have joyfully beaten to death the entire National Assembly, they would have kissed the King's feet, if he had let them forget just once, for one hour, their hunger and their barren despair.

And they pressed their noses flat against the iron bars of the fences, they stuck their hands through them, hordes of beggars, crowds of moaning pariahs. And their terrible stench floated into the park like a sinister crimson cloud, heralding a dawn of terror. They had clung to the fences like horrifying spiders, and their eyes had roamed far into the park over the serene lawns, the gates, the laurel groves, the marble statues which sweetly smiling looked down on them from their pedestals. Cute little love gods, plump as fattened geese, with arms

like white overstuffed sausages, aimed their arrows of love at
their wide open mouths and beckoned them with a stone
quiver, while the hand of the bailiffs, who had come to throw
them into the debtors' prisons, fell on their shoulders like a
block of wood.

The sleepers groaned, and those who were awake envied
them their sleep.

High above them in the cold October sky went the iron
plow of time, which tilled its fields with grief, sowed them
with want, so that out of them one day the flame of revenge
would rise, so that one day the arms of these thousands would
grow light, soaring and gay like doves, when the guillotine
knives served the Reaper, so that one day they could walk
like gods under the sky, bare headed, in the eternal Whitsun
of an endless dawn.

From the whitish sky at the far end of the highway a black
dot detached itself.

Those in front saw it, they drew each other's attention to
it. Those who slept awoke and jumped up. Everyone looked
down the road. Was this black dot the Mecca of their hope,
was it their salvation?

For a short moment they all believed it, they forced themselves to believe it.

But the dot grew too rapidly. Now they all saw that it was
not the slow progress of many carts, it was not a flour
caravan. And hope lost itself in the wind and left their brow.

But who was that? Who rode so wildly? Who, in this dead
time, had a reason to ride like that?

A few men climbed the thick willows and peered over the
heads of the masses.

Now they saw him and shouted his name. It was Maillard.
Maillard of the Bastille. Maillard of the Fourteenth of July.

He kept going until he was in the midst of the crowd.
Then he pulled up, capable of uttering but one word. "Treachery!" he shouted.

Thereupon the hurricane broke loose. "Treachery, treachery!" Some ten men grabbed hold of him and lifted him up
on their shoulders. He stood aloft, supporting himself with
one hand against a tree, faint with exertion, almost blinded
by the sweat which ran out of his black hair into his eyes.

"Maillard wants to speak," the word went around. Then a
terrible stillness set in. Everyone waited in the terrible seconds
in which the future of France was weighed, till the scale

full of fetters, dungeons, crosses, bibles, rosaries, crowns, scepters, orbs, embedded in the false gentleness of bourbon lilies, full of empty words, promises, lists full of broken royal oaths, unjust verdicts, ruthless privileges, this monstrous mountain of everything with which the centuries had deceived Europe, slowly began to sink.

Maillard swung himself up into the tree.

Down from his leafless pulpit he flung his terrible words across the people, across the barren fields, the gloomy ramparts, the black drawbridges overloaded with people, into the vaults of the jails, across the roofs of Paris, into the yards and alleys of the dismal faubourgs, into the remote citadels of misery under the earth, where the damned lived in the sewers among the rats.

"To the nation! You poor people, you wretched people, you outcasts! You are being betrayed. You are being squeezed out. Soon you will walk around naked, you will die in the streets, and from your stiff hands the tax-lessees, the myrmidons of Capet, bloodhounds of the bloodhound, spiders of the spider, will wrench your last penny.

"We have been deserted, we have been disowned, and the end is drawing near. Soon they shall rip our last coat from our bodies. They shall make us nooses out of our shirts. Our bodies shall plaster the roads, so that the hangman's carriage keeps its wheels clean. And why shouldn't we die? We defile the air with our bodies, we stink, we are untouchable, isn't that the truth? Why shouldn't we die? What can we do about it anyway? Can we even think of defending ourselves? We have been crushed, we have been gagged.

"They have willfully created famines, they have starved us, starvation has killed us."

Each word fell like a heavy brick among the people. With every syllable Maillard threw his arms forward, as if he wanted to jolt the very horizon with the bombardment of his words.

"Do you know what happened last night?

"The Queen—"

"Ah, the Queen," and the crowds became quieter still, when they heard the hated name.

"The Queen, do you know what that old whore has done? She has ordered three dragoon regiments to Versailles. They are quartered in all the houses, and the members of the Assembly hardly dare say a word, Mirabeau has shrunk to the size of a dwarf, and all the others can scarcely muster enough courage to clear their throats. It is a disgrace to watch. What did they swear in the Ballroom, these comedians of liberty? What did you spill your blood for at the Bastille? It was all in vain, do you hear, in vain.

"You have to crawl back into your holes again, the torch of liberty has turned into a tiny night light, a dim, miserable train-oil lamp. Good enough to light your way back to your dens.

"In three days' time Broglie will be here with his troops. The Assembly will be sent home, the rack set up again. The Bastille will be rebuilt. The taxes paid again. Even now the jaws of all the dungeons are gaping.

"Your hunger will not be stilled, despair to your hearts' content. The King has had the breadcarts seized before they reached Orleans and has sent them home again."

Maillard's words were drowned in a shout of anger. A throng of clenched fists shook itself in the air. The crowds began to whirl, like a monstrous maelstrom, around his tree.

And the tree towered out of the sea of shouts, out of the swirl of distorted faces, and an echo of wrath which rebounded from the sky like a black enormous whirlwind shook it like the booming clapper of an iron bell.

High above in the leaden branches Maillard hung like an enormous black bird and threw his arms hither and thither in a circle, as if he wanted to prepare himself to fly over the crowds of people, out into the evening, a demon of despair, a black Belial, the God of the masses, sowing sombre fire with his hands.

Out of the raging crowd suddenly a loud voice rang out twice, in the paroxysm of a piercing treble, with the call: "To Versailles, to Versailles!" It was, as if the enormous crowd itself had called, as if one will had pronounced what stirred in these thousands of minds. Now they knew their goal. There was no longer chaos, the mob instantaneously changed into a mighty army. The western sky like an enormous magnet, twisted their heads round to where Versailles awaited them. The forces which the storm of despair had unearthed in them now had an aim. The dam had broken.

The first rows spontaneously began to march, four or five abreast, as many as the width of the street permitted.

Maillard saw that. He climbed down out of his tree as fast as he could, called three men whom he knew, and ran with them over the fields alongside the masses. When he had overtaken them, he tried to make them stop, to persuade them that they should choose a leader, get arms. But they did not listen to him. Now his voice was as powerless as anyone else's to halt these iron batallions. The masses pushed him aside, they overran the feeble barricade formed by the four men and tore Maillard and his people with them down the street.

Men and women, laborers, students, lawyers, in white wigs, knickerbockers and sansculottes, ladies of the market, fishmongers, women with children in their arms, city soldiers, who swung their pikes over the crowd like generals, cobblers with leather aprons and wooden shoes, tailors, innkeepers, beggars, vagabonds, ragged and torn, all welded together in the fire of their enthusiasm.

That was the evening, when the slave, the serf of the centuries, threw off his chains and lifted up his head in the setting sun, a Prometheus, carrying a new fire in his hands.

They were unarmed, what did that matter, they were without a commander, what of it? Where was hunger now, where misery?

They marched hand in hand, they embraced each other. They had not suffered in vain. They all knew that the years of suffering were over, and their hearts trembled softly.

An eternal melody filled the sky and its purple blueness, an eternal torch burnt. And the sun pulled them ahead, down into the evening, it lit up the forests, it burnt the sky. And like divine ships, manned with the spirits of freedom, big clouds sailed ahead of them in the rapid winds.

And the enormous poplars along the road shone like great candelabras, each tree a golden flame, lighting the course of their fame.

This story is based on the historical events leading to the march of the Parisian masses on the royal palace at Versailles, which took place on October 5, 1789, and which *The Cambridge Modern History* describes as follows:

On the morning of October 5 a crowd, in the first instance chiefly of women, although afterwards supported by men, assembled in the Place de Grève and began an assault on the Hôtel de Ville. Feebly resisted by the National Guards on duty, they forced their way in, seized a quantity of arms and were about to hang an Abbé whom they chanced to find there, when a certain Stanislas Maillard, who had taken part in the attack on the Bastille, raised the cry "To Versailles." The women followed him, and on the march were joined by crowds of male rioters.

Beside the historical source, "The Fifth of October" also reflects the influence of two authors Heym greatly admired. There are some similarities with Grabbe's play *Napoleon or The Hundred Days* (*Napoleon oder die hundert Tage*), in which the crowds are as antagonistic to bakers as those in "The Fifth of October." In both works allegations are made that the famine has been brought about intentionally by those in power. The Parisian market-women are designated as "Damen der Halle" in the play as well as in the story. The episode of the baker in "The Fifth of October," which replaces the historic incident with the cleric in the Hôtel de Ville, is further reminiscent of a scene in Grabbe's play, in which a tailor is murdered by ruffians from the faubourg St. Antoine. It lacks a "happy ending," but otherwise the circumstances are comparable. Concrete evidence of the connection between the two works lies in the fact that the coal-carriers who wanted to kill the baker also hailed from St. Antoine.

But this episode from "The Fifth of October" shows a still closer resemblance to the scene from Büchner's play *Danton's Death* (*Dantons Tod*) in which the mob threatens to hang a young aristocrat. In view of Heym's great admiration for Büchner there is little doubt that his baker was a direct descendant of this figure. However, the similarity of "The Fifth of October" with *Danton's Death* goes beyond such details and extends to the underlying fatalistic outlook of the respective authors. Büchner uses Danton as a mouthpiece for his historical fatalism in these remarks: "We have not made the Revolution, but the Revolution has made us," and "We are puppets whose strings are pulled by unknown powers; nothing, nothing are we ourselves!" In a letter to his betrothed, written in spring, 1834, Büchner stressed the pointlessness of opposing the "iron law" of history—a viewpoint which recurs in Schnitzler, particularly in *The Green Cockatoo* (*Der grüne Kakadu*).

Deviating from his historical source, Heym used Maillard to demonstrate the individual's subjection to the law of historical necessity. Actually, this Bastille veteran took the initiative in the march on the royal residence, and placed himself at the head of the marchers. According to Heym, however, Maillard was a prophet of gloom and a defeatist. When the demonstrators got under way he vainly tried to halt their march by arguments and action, but he and his handful of helpers were swept away by the people. Maillard is shown to be utterly incapable of influencing or guiding the course of events. His impotence in the face of the people's decision to march on Versailles implies that in the storming of the Bastille he had been a mere tool of fate, a puppet manipulated by the unknown forces that rule the universe. If Maillard in the story "The Fifth of October" is thus a clear and straightforward embodiment of Heym's basic outlook on the world, the role of the people in this work is much more complicated. Almost up to the last page the misery and hopelessness of life in the Parisian proletarian quarters are depicted with ever increasing penetration. But when Captain Maillard shatters the people's last hope of a better future, an almost forcible turn takes place in the action of the story. Instead of showing definite resignation, the people allow themselves to be stung into action by an anonymous shout.

The fact that from this turning point on the people are attributed with the power and the will to revolt against their fate may seem at first sight to be inconsistent with Heym's conception of humanity as a creature driven passively by demonic forces. On closer consideration it appears that the discrepancy is limited to the surface, because the turn in the development of the action affects the function of the collective protagonist. Initially the Parisians by their misery and helplessness demonstrate the absolute subjection of humanity to a gruesome fate. In the last sections of the story they offer the same demonstration, for they themselves represent the forces of fate in their relations to Maillard and his people.

The apparent optimism of the closing images is, moreover, ironically ambiguous. The people are compared with Prometheus who brought fire from the gods, but was afterwards chained to a rock where an eagle devoured his liver. As the people marched on Versailles, they "knew" the years of suffering were over. History proved them wrong. In the years of revolution and terror which followed, their lot became even worse, and with the advent of Napoleon—for whom Heym had limitless admiration—the revolution was virtually abrogated. But the story does not merely indirectly show the fatuity of the hopes which moved the Parisian masses at the outset of the French Revolution. Like all individuals who appear in Heym's work, they represent the whole of humanity. The glaring unhistoricity of the concluding scene therefore unmasks the illusiveness of all idealistic dreams of a better world to come. Thus, "The Fifth of October" does indeed in every respect appear to be most typical of the pessimistic, fatalistic conception of human existence to which Heym subscribed.

Of the other works in Heym's collection of prose, the most interesting is the title story "The Thief" ("Der Dieb") which concludes the book. Like "The Fifth of October," "The Thief" is based on an actual occurrence, although in this case it was a contemporary rather than a historic event. The theft in August, 1911, of the "Mona Lisa" from the Parisian Louvre provided Heym with the basic idea and the setting of the story. But of the actual incident, only the broadest outline went into the making of Heym's work. Nor could it be otherwise, because the crime was not solved until twenty-three months after his death. All Heym had to go on were the more or less fanciful newspaper descriptions of the discovery of the theft.

Probably because the picture originated in Florence, Heym placed the denouement of his fictitious account in that city, in the future year 1914. By coincidence it was there that on December 12, 1913, the painting was recovered. Apart from this, there is no resemblance between Heym's reconstruction of the incident and the actual course of events.

Instead of the youthful Italian decorator Vincenzo Perugia, ex-employee of the Louvre, who claimed to have acted from an excess of nationalist zeal, Heym introduced as the thief an elderly religious maniac who was prompted by his delusions and hallucinations. And whereas the portrait was finally restored to the museum unharmed, he made the thief destroy it in a frenzy of hatred.

Nevertheless, Heym's version of the theft and its aftermath is not pure invention. Several essential elements in it are based on an incident which took place half a year before the "Mona Lisa" affair. On January 13, 1911, the Rembrandt painting known as the "Nightwatch" was damaged in the Rijksmuseum in Amsterdam. An unemployed ship's cook, H. Sigrist, attacked the picture with a cobbler's knife, but before he could do more than scratch the surface of the thick layer of varnish and dirt which then covered it, the museum guards intervened. Although the "Nightwatch" escaped virtually unscathed, the European press published faked photographs designed to give an exaggerated impression of the extent of the damage. These were accompanied by articles written in highly sensational tones: "AN UNHEARD OF INFAMY has been perpetrated in Amsterdam on one of the very greatest masterpieces ever created by Man. In the famous State Museum there the magnificent, the sublime Rembrandt-painting The Nightwatch has been severely damaged by knife cuts!"[1] It seems likely that these accounts of the "Nightwatch" incident contributed more to "The Thief" than did the theft of the "Mona Lisa." Sigrist was said to have been insane; the behavior of Heym's protagonist, who is referred to as "the crazy one" and "the lunatic," is typical of a schizoid personality with paranoid trends. For the attack on the Rembrandt painting a knife was used. The same type of weapon served the thief in the story to mutilate the portrait of Mona Lisa.

Once Heym, influenced by the occurrence in Amsterdam, adopted madness as the motive force behind the theft, he was forced to reject the only concrete fact known about the stealing of the "Mona Lisa." Heym's thief suffers from a religious mania, which ultimately attaches itself to the painting of "La Gioconda" as the symbol of evil. The thief feels the presence of legions of devils who lurk behind it, waiting for the moment when they will burst forth from it to conquer the world. He has been told by an angel of the Lord that he is to save mankind by destroying the picture. As all the forces of evil are concentrated in it, even to touch the frame is an audacity fraught with the most terrible dangers. As a consequence the thief stands in terrified awe of the portrait.*

This being the case, Heym could not let the protagonist of his tale, like Vincenzo Perugia, tackle the painting quite disrespectfully with a set of carpenters' tools to remove glass and frame, and then roll up the canvas to hide it under his coat. For the sake of the integrity of his story and in keeping with the feelings of fear he ascribed to the thief, Heym made him wrap painting and frame intact in a parcel which the guards were accustomed to see him carry.

Long before the disappearance of da Vinci's masterpiece Heym

---

*Thomas Mann's story, "Gladius Dei," from the collection *Tristan,* also deals with a religious maniac who regards a certain painting as evil and wants to destroy it. *Tristan* appeared in 1903, so it is possible that Heym knew this story. There are no indications, however, that "The Thief" owes anything directly to "Gladius Dei."

was familiar with the painting, its background, and the various legends attached to it. He gained his knowledge from Mereschkowski's romanticized biography of the painter, which was one of his favorite books. This work has left its mark on "The Thief" in several ways. In the chapter devoted to the portrait of Mona Lisa, Mereschkowski hints darkly at its magical qualities and dwells on the irresistible beauty of its subject. This may well have played a part in determining Heym's conception of the picture as teeming with demons and of its thief as succumbing to its seductive charms, for which he denounces even his God. Another link between Mereschkowski's *Leonardo da Vinci* and Heym's "The Thief" is established by the occurrence of the same Biblical quotations from Mark 15 and Revelation 17.

"The Thief" is not only much longer than the other works in the collection, but also much more complicated in structure. The development and prehistory of the mania which incites the protagonist to the theft of the "Mona Lisa" are, after a brief introductory passage, depicted in the form of an extensive flashback. When the thief has stolen the painting, the poet quite literally passes over an interval of three years by means of a dash. The original religious mania which caused the protagonist to see in the portrait the embodiment of evil has in the meantime given way to a passionate love for the painting. But Mona Lisa seems to mock the thief on account of his feelings, and thus provokes him to the act of revenge through which the final catastrophe is brought about.

The thematic transition from the religious to the erotic sphere is a consistent and psychological development of the action. His hatred of the feminine sex, which in the first part causes the thief to see in the portrait of La Gioconda a symbol of evil, is only a religiously disguised aspect of his ambivalent attitude toward the opposite sex. It is very much to the point here to refer to Freud's theories, according to which religion belongs to those phenomena which have their origin in the Oedipus complex.[2] Thereby religion is closely related to such difficulties in the libidinal economy as manifest themselves in the fetishistic and ambivalent attitude of the thief to the "Mona Lisa." Heym obviously knew something about psychoanalytic theory.[3] It is significant, for instance, that in "The Thief" typical symbols like snakes and umbrellas occur. Moreover, the thief protects himself against the regard of La Gioconda through phallic gestures or by carrying a silver phallus. His initial religiously disguised hatred of the painting thus in many ways reveals itself as a perverted love, which in the second part of the story appears in a more direct form.

But whether it appears as love or hate, the maniac's attitude to the painting is the outcome of his condition, in which his human reason and judgment have been superseded by a demonic force. How completely he is enslaved and possessed by this power, which he believes is divine, becomes clear in the description of his final acceptance of his mission: "He lay before God in the dust, he humiliated himself, he tore his entire soul apart and let God stream in like smoke, like a fluid. . . . And on the tips of his hands which he swung in the dark a weak blue light gleamed like a St. Elmo's fire, as if God's power entered into him like an electric current to fill him with ecstasy." The dehumanizing effect of the thief's submission to a superior force is accentuated in his animal-like behavior and appearance when he is about to steal the painting: "He let himself down on his hands, and so he crawled on all fours like an animal through the anteroom. . . ."

In "The Lunatic" Heym makes much more extensive use of this animalization motif. An irresistible force takes possession of the human being and determines his actions so completely that he at last seems to lose his human shape and begins to embody this demonic force: "He felt that anger wanted to rise up in him again. He was afraid of this dark madness. Phew, now it will grab me again in a moment, he thought. He was dizzy, he held on to a tree and closed his eyes. Suddenly he saw the animal that was in him again. Down between the entrails like a large hyena. Some jaws that animal had. And the dirty bastard wanted to get out. Yes, yes, you have to get out.

"Now he himself was the animal, and on all fours he crawled along the street. . . . His long mane flew, his claws hit in the air, and his tongue hung out of his mouth."

Later in this story the lunatic is again completely overpowered by his madness. The autonomy of thought and action, which according to traditional humanistic ideas typifies the human being, is lost. His demonic possession is once again symbolized through an external metamorphosis into the shape of an animal. The metamorphosis here too is introduced through a feeling of weakness and by closing of the eyes. Then the madman changes into the animal shape embodying the powers which dominate him:

"He was a large white bird over a large lonely ocean, cradled by eternal brightness, high up in the blue."

A brief survey of the other stories collected in *The Thief* indicates that they, too, in different ways express Heym's pessimistic fatalism concerning mankind's position in the universe. In the story "Jonathan" the poet's conception of human fate is illustrated by a fatally injured ship's engineer. The fact that this man is the passive toy of higher powers is made clear through his life story, the course of which has completely eluded his own will or control. Moreover, sickness and death are depicted in a way, and with the aid of a terminology, which accentuates human passivity, helplessness, and subjugation to fate.

Thus Heym writes of the sick in general: "And they had to lie quietly in their beds, they had to give themselves up to physical pain, they were flayed alive, oh," and of Jonathan in particular: "Fever overpowered him with all its violence. . . . When he woke up the pain in his legs overtook him with such force that he became almost unconscious." The last scenes in which the visions of the dying man are depicted show his defenselessness against the power of death. The traditional allegorical skeleton beckons Jonathan who is forced to follow him into the realm of death.

In "The Ship" ("Das Schiff") the inexorable, inescapable fate of the crew of a small sailing ship appears to them in the form of a plague. Throughout the story the author stresses the mental and physical paralysis which overcomes the crew when confronted with its fate. The theme of the absolute subjection of humanity by demonic forces is expressed with particular clearness in the following sentences: "Immediately they all realized in the same moment that they were lost. They were in the merciless hands of a terrible invisible foe. . . ."

"An Afternoon" ("Ein Nachmittag") distinguishes itself from these works in that this "contribution to the biography of a small boy" in no way deals with extreme characters or situations. In the framework of this work the insignificance and vulnerability of mankind in the face of the forces of fate is, however, clearly noticeable. Apart from significant expressions like "Then torment overpowered him," one finds the completely unmistakable remark that the protagonist was "condemned . . . still often to be shaken by the extremes of the deepest torments and the wildest happiness." In this story Heym shows that mankind's passive sufferance of fate does not occur only in such extraordinary cases as he represents in his other works. Even in the everyday realm of childish hopes and disappointments and against the banal background of a bourgeois seaside resort, the human existence is shown to be guided by forces which are completely beyond the influence of the creature.

In "The Dissection" ("Die Sektion") the passivity of the main figure is of course already determined by the given situation, namely that a corpse is being dissected. The dehumanization which is derived from this is further stressed in the description of the doctors' activities: "Over their hands the blood ran, and they dipped them ever deeper into the cold corpse and took its contents out, like white cooks who gut a goose." The dead man "patiently let himself be pulled to and fro, be jerked to and fro by his hair." Fritz Martini has expressed the opinion that the occurrence of the motif of love in this story amounts to a departure from Heym's customary absolute pessimism because it introduces a force capable of conquering death and decay.[4] This interpretation is not entirely convincing. Rather than adding a new dimension to the story, the motif of love seems to be a consistent development of the theme which in the first half of the story is deployed in its physical aspects. The first part of this very short work describes how after death the human body seems to come to life once again—on a subhuman level—through the process of decay: "Beautiful red and blue colors" cause the corpse to resemble "a shimmering calyx, a mysterious plant from Indian jungles."

In the second half of the story the apparent blossoming of the corpse extends to the brain. The distortion of the putrifying lips suggests smiling and kissing. This description offers a means of attributing to the macabre revitalizing effect of decay the spiritual expression demanded in this context through the vehicle of a dream of love. "The Dissection" thus appears to be entirely consistent with Heym's characteristic use of death and decay to demonstrate his fatalistic world view.

From this survey of the stories in Heym's collection *The Thief*, it becomes clear that his prose does not offer much basis of comparison with his contemporaries. His stories are a highly personal literary sublimation of the sociological conditions common to all representatives of the expressionist generation. The peculiar composition of Heym's personality and the particular nature of his creative talent account for the unique qualities of these works which distinguish them from other prose *oeuvres* springing from the same substratum.

The other authors of this era, such as Albert Ehrenstein, Robert Musil, Ernst Blass, and Ferdinand Hardekopf, whatever their mutual differences, all shared a preoccupation with the minute analysis of the individual mind as the motive force of behavior. Not so Heym: The behavior of his characters reveals no individual, but a general human pattern, which is determined not by personal traits, but by the dreaded onslaught of the inescapable forces of fate.

8

A Rebel in Retrospect

THE QUINTESSENCE of Georg Heym's work may be summarized, on the basis of the findings of the present study, as a denial of the anthropocentric conception of life. Heym created a universe in which man is not the supreme force capable of dominating and exploiting the world for his own materialistic purposes through his rational powers. In his works, a deanimated humanity, reduced to utter insignificance in the cosmic order, is the passive victim of demonized natural and metaphysical phenomena. This hopeless pessimism determines the tone of practically all his writings. There are, to be sure, occasional images of great beauty and serenity in his work. An example of this is the stanza which concludes a depressing and dehumanizing depiction of a "Garden Party" ("Laubenfest").

> Im blauen Abend steht Gewölke weit,
> Delphinen mit den rosa Flossen gleich,
> Die schlafen in der Meere Einsamkeit.
>
> (In the blue evening clouds are everywhere,
> Like dolphins with pink fins,
> Which swim in the loneliness of the seas.)

Such instances of relief from the gloom and horror of Heym's customary poetic visions are relatively rare, and they do no more than hint at the possibility of some ideal in which mankind could free its existence from the misery and horror of fate's absolute domination. Yet these restrainedly positive passages are a very essential part of his work and establish his relationship with the expressionist movement.[1] However, in the overall effect of his *oeuvre* these proto-idealistic elements tend to be completely overshadowed by the much more prominent and characteristic atmosphere of dismal hopelessness.

The pessimistic fatalism and negativism which thus dominate Heym's work contrast sharply with the essential optimism of most other leading expressionists, in whose writings the idealistic aspect was generally far more stressed than the negatively critical one. Unlike Heym, for whom the destruction of the prevailing world image was the main object, they did not regard the attack on the established values and institutions as an end in itself. To them, it was only a preliminary step—be it a highly important one—to the evocation of visions of a new and better world to take the place of the old.

The evidence of post-1945 literature suggests strongly that Georg Heym's almost complete lack of idealistic tendencies is more congenial to the outlook of the atomic era than the often aggressive idealism of most other expressionists. This consonance is probably a major factor in the current preference for Heym. The predominant attitude of post-World-War-II literature in this respect is represented by Max Frisch's radio play, *Mr. Biedermann and the Incendiaries* (*Herr Biedermann und die Brandstifter*), which was first performed in 1953.[2]

In this work the problems of idealism and faith in mankind are central issues. At the last dinner which he and his wife Babette offer their strange guests, Biedermann makes a plea for mutual confidence:

> Didn't I always say so, Babette: my acquaintances should speak their minds, I am Gottlieb Biedermann, I believe in mankind. Only faith from man to man—
> (*A bottle is opened*)
> Only faith, I say—. Why does everyone live only in his little cliques, dear God, we simply don't know each other, why don't we talk together? Everyone takes everyone else for an arsonist or what not; instead of offering each other our hands.

Or am I not right? A little bit of idealism, my friends, a little
bit of good will and things like that—   (page 31)

The spuriousness of Biedermann's idealism is revealed on two
levels: in his particular case, as well as in general terms. In one
of the author's announcements, which interrupt the action from
time to time, he gives the following interpretation of his work:
"Here, I believe, it is not a matter of depicting divine punishment,
but simply of depicting an average middle-class citizen, who has
rather a bad conscience (in my opinion, as I said, with good
reason) and who would like to have an easy conscience: without
changing anything. That is of course only possible by lying to
oneself, and that is what makes him dangerous." Biedermann's
idealistic confidence in his guests is insincere self-deception, and
since on the author's evidence he represents the average citizen,
all idealism found among the great majority of mankind is herewith marked as a lie.

Up to this point the accent lies on the element of social and
moral criticism in Frisch's treatment of the question of idealism.
However, he does not stop at this but demonstrates that the guests
were really not worthy of any confidence, even if it had been
inspired by genuine idealism, because they *are* in fact incendiaries
and will ultimately destroy the city. Herewith the basis for all
idealistic visions of universal brotherhood and all faith in the
essential goodness of man's nature has been destroyed, because
it can no longer be maintained that a pernicious outward order
is responsible for distorting man's originally good nature. The guilt
lies in mankind itself, and renders it defenseless against, or even
causes it to lend assistance to, the evil forces which are bent on its
destruction. Herewith Frisch is essentially in agreement with
Heym, and his Biedermann is a close relative of the human beings
in the latter's works*

Biedermann's guilt is seen by Max Frisch in psychological terms
which were foreign to Georg Heym. Nevertheless to the latter,
too, mankind is in the final analysis guilty and deserving of the

---

*Biedermann's "terrible fear" (p. 25) corresponds very closely to the basic
element in Heym's work which Karl Ludwig Schneider describes as follows:
"The knowledge of pronouncedly primordial fear is a central experience of
Heym and one of the starting points for an understanding of his entire work"
—*Der bildhafte Ausdruck in den Dichtungen Georg Heyms, Georg Trakls und
Ernst Stadlers* (Heidelberg, 1954), p. 35.

punishment it receives, as is expressed most clearly in the Biblical terminology of the final stanza of "The War." Fritz Martini writes in this context, "And what at first appears only as diabolical destruction, is consummated as a judgment over Sodom and Gomorrah, an indication that the demonic act of the diabolical forces was also experienced and accepted as necessary justice."[3]

But although Heym chose an Old-Testamentarian image to imply that mankind bears a guilt which provokes terrible punishment, this guilt cannot be of a religious nature, if only because the retribution does not emanate from God but from a cruel and unknowable fate. In this context it is revealing that Heym wrote in his diary, "undoubtedly the idea of an amoral fate is more profound than that of a moral . . . God" (6.26.1910). The profundity of this thought lay for him in the consideration that a moral God would mete out his chastisement only to those who had violated His commands—that there would be a direct relationship between human disobedience and divine wrath. This was contrary to his observation that people often were much unhappier than their course of conduct seemed to justify. Moreover, defiance of God would presume an independence and initiative which the utterly will-less, dehumanized creatures in Heym's poetic universe simply do not possess. It seemed much more consistent with his views to postulate an amoral fate as the source of the relentless arbitrary persecution to which mankind is exposed—regardless of individual virtues and vices.

This does not mean that the allusion to human guilt in "The War" is without significance as far as Heym's world image is concerned. Neither is it a mere by-product of a motif introduced for its spectacular qualities without regard to its implications. In a diary entry Heym confirms that mankind's unhappiness is the consequence of guilt: "Why are we so unhappy, what are we guilty of?" In the same note he speaks of "our unknown guilt" (6.7.1907). There is only one kind of guilt which could be attributed to humanity as Heym saw it: a completely passive acceptance of its lot, an apathetic suffering of a destiny over which it has not the slightest control. Its only attribute is its existence, and therefore that alone can consititute its guilt.

This existential guilt is only negatively related to Heidegger's conception of guilt, insofar as it has no reference to theology or any system of morals. For Heidegger, the human being as such is guilty, because man cannot choose to realize all possibilities of his existence. According to Heym, man has, to use Heidegger's terminology, no existence, only facticity. Man's existence does not offer him any possibilities or choice, and he is simply guilty because he is. This applies to all men, because in his poetic cosmos Heym does not admit any distinctions; all men are equal in their absolute subordination to fate. Herein lies the difference between his idea of guilt and that of Kafka, who also held that human existence per se is culpable, but who limited this to one specific social class, the bourgeoisie. Thus Karl Rossmann in *Amerika* is innocent,* in contrast to K. who is "completely absorbed by the spheres of business and bourgeois conformity." K. "represents the average middle-class citizen of modern society. For that very reason he is guilty. . . ." His "exclusively bourgeois existence" is "his real guilt."4

The inescapable universality and absoluteness of Heym's guilt concept may be a contributing factor in his rising repute. It bridges the half century since his death, with its wars, concentration camps, gas chambers, and nuclear bombs, and gives him a frightening actuality in this "Time of Guilty Men" (*Zeit der Schuldigen*). He anticipated the lesson which subsequent generations drew from the catastrophes which have engulfed the world since his death: "Guilt is something as general as an eclipse of the sun: it applies to everyone."5

*Heinz Politzer, in his *Franz Kafka. Parable and Paradox* (Ithaca: Cornell University Press, 1962), disagrees with the common view that Rossmann is guiltless.

Notes

Introduction

1. F. J. Schneider, *Der expressive Mensch und die deutsche Lyrik der Gegenwart* (Stuttgart, 1927), p. 134.

2. B. J. Kenworthy, *Georg Kaiser* (Oxford, 1957), pp. 152-53. See also Richard Brinkmann, *Forschungs-Probleme*, p. 60.

3. Otto Mann in *Expressionismus. Gestalten einer literarischen Bewegung*, ed. Hermann Friedmann and Otto Mann (Heidelberg, 1956), pp. 264-79.

4. Wolfgang Paulsen, *Georg Kaiser* (Tübingen, 1960). See Brinkmann, p. 91.

5. Brinkmann, p. 63.

6. *Lyrik des expressionistischen Jahrzehnts. Von den Wegbereitern bis zum Dada*, with an Introduction by Gottfried Benn (Wiesbaden, 1955).

7. *Die Lyrik des Expressionismus. Voraussetzungen. Ergebnisse und Grenzen. Nachwirkungen*, ed. Clemens Heselhaus, *Deutsche Texte* 5 (Tübingen, 1956).

8. This best known and most authoritative anthology of poetry of the expressionist era is again available—*Menschheitsdämmerung. Ein Dokument des Expressionismus*, ed. Kurt Pinthus, newly revised edition (Hamburg, 1959).

9. Albert Soergel and Curt Hohoff, *Dichtung und Dichter der Zeit. Vom Naturalismus bis zur Gegenwart*, II (Düsseldorf, 1963).

10. *Georg Heym, Dichtungen und Schriften*, collected edition, ed. Karl Ludwig Schneider: *Tagebücher Träume Briefe*, Vol. III (Hamburg, Munich, 1960); *Prosa und Dramen*, Vol. II (1962); *Lyrik*, Vol. I (1964).

11. See Karl Ludwig Schneider, "Anspruchsvolle Fehldeutungen. Anmerkungen zu einer Heym-Monographie von Kurt Mautz," *Die Zeit* (January 19, 1962). Mautz' book appeared in Frankfurt/M, Bonn, 1961.

12. Eduard Spranger, *Die Psychologie des Jugendalters* (Leipzig, 1929).

13. *Style and Society in German Literary Expressionism*, University of Florida Monographs, Humanities Series XV (Gainesville, 1964).

CHAPTER 1

1. See letter 5 from Georg Heym to the Reifeprüfungskommission des Friedrich-Wilhelms-Gymnasiums, and the diary note of 12.31.1910, both in *Dichtungen und Schriften*, III. See also Helmut Greulich, *Georg Heym, 1887-1912. Leben und Werk* (Berlin, 1931), pp. 9-10.

2. Georg Reicke, "Die Groszstadt," *Die Neue Rundschau* (February, 1912), pp. 202 ff; Conrad Bornhak, *Deutsche Geschichte unter Kaiser Wilhelm II* (Leipzig, Erlangen, 1922), pp. 181, 205; Martin Göhring, *Bismarcks Erben 1890-1945* (Wiesbaden, 1958), p. 25.

3. Hans Heinrich Muchow, *Sexualreife und Sozialstruktur der Jugend* (Hamburg, 1959), p. 54.

4. *Ibid.*, pp. 53-54.

5. Franz Werfel, *Nicht der Mörder, der Ermordete ist schuldig* (Munich, Leipzig, 1920), p. 99.

6. Kurt Wais, *Das Vater-Sohn-Motiv in der Dichtung* (Berlin, Leipzig, 1931), II, Introduction.

7. *Die Neue Rundschau*, Vol. 63, No. 2 (1952), pp. 191 ff.

8. First version of the work in *Sämtliche Werke und ausgewählte Briefe* (Munich, 1956), I, 738.

9. Greulich, p. 9.

10. See Carl Seelig in *Georg Heym, Gesammelte Gedichte*, ed. C. Seelig (Zürich, 1947), p. 202. See also Mautz, pp. 258-59.

CHAPTER 2

1. Fr. Thiersch, quoted in Theobald Ziegler, *Die geistigen und sozialen Strömungen Deutschlands im 19. und 20. Jahrhundert* (Berlin, 1916), p. 538.

2. Stefan Zweig, *Die Welt von Gestern* (Frankfurt/M, 1949), p. 50.

3. Heinrich Begemann, *Friedrich-Wilhelms-Gymnasium zu Neu-Ruppin. Bericht über das Schuljahr 1905/6* (Neu-Ruppin, 1906). See also the report for 1906/7, published in 1907.

4. See, for instance, Ludwig Gurlitt, *Der Deutsche und seine Schule* (Berlin, 1906), and H. Keller, *Jugend und Erziehung in der modernen deutschen Dichtung* (Lachen, 1938).

5. Bornhak, p. 24.

6. *Dienstanweisung für die Direktoren und Lehrer an den höheren Lehranstalten für die männliche Jugend.* This directive of December 12, 1910, issued by the Prussian education minister, is quoted in the annual report 1910/11 of the Friedrich-Wilhelms-Gymnasium.

7. Julius Langbehn, *Rembrandt als Erzieher. Von einem Deutschen* (Leipzig, 1922), p. 51.

8. *Ibid.*, p. 45.

9. Robert Hessen, "Zur Hygiene des Schülerselbstmords," *Die Neue Rundschau* (September, 1911), p. 1295.

10. 2.8.1905, 4.23.1905, 6.5.1905, 7.16.1905, 10.31.1905, 5.25.1906, 6.14.1906, 8.6.1906, 9.20.1906, 10.18.1906, 11.11.1906, 1.8.1907.

11. *Schulordnung für das Friedrich-Wilhelms-Gymnasium und seine Vorschule zu Neu-Ruppin*, dated January 20, 1908.

12. 10.21.1907, 12.16.1907, 3.4.1909, 5.18.1909, 10.8.1909, 9.2.1911.

13. 6.14.1905; see also 6.17.1905, 6.24.1905.

14. See Hermann Hesse, *Demian* (Berlin, 1922), p. 97.

15. Zweig, p. 87.

16. Spranger, p. 314.
17. Hans Bethge, *Hölderlin* (Berlin, Leipzig, n.d.), p. 19.
18. *Friedrich Hölderlin, Sämtliche Werke*, ed. Friedrich Beissner, Vol. I, No. 2 (Stuttgart, 1943), p. 485.

CHAPTER 3

1. Carl Seelig, "Leben und Sterben von Georg Heym," *Gesammelte Gedichte*, p. 230.
2. See the retrospective notes of 3.4.1909 and 9.2.1911.
3. 11.18.1910; see also 9.26.1910, 10.22.1910, 11.3.1910, 11.28.1910, 11.29.1910.
4. *Expressionismus. Literatur und Kunst 1910-1923*, Eine Ausstellung des deutschen Literaturarchivs im Schiller-Nationalmuseum, Marbach a.N. vom 8. Mai bis 31. Oktober, 1960 (Sonderausstellungen des Schiller-Nationalmuseums, Katalog Nr. 7), ed. Bernhard Zeller, pp. 23-24. For a detailed examination of the history of the Neue Club and its subsidiary enterprise Das Neopathetische Cabaret, and of Heym's relations with them, see my article, "Georg Heym und der Neue Club," *Revista de Letras* (Assis), IV (1963), 262-71.
5. *Jakob van Hoddis, Weltende. Gesammelte Dichtungen*, ed. Paul Pörtner (Zürich, 1958), p. 143.
6. Kurt Hiller, *Die Weisheit der Langenweile. Eine Zeit- und Streitschrift* (Leipzig, 1913), I, 119.
7. *Ibid.*, p. 120.
8. E. L. [Edwin Loewenson], quoted in *Weltende*, p. 143.
9. See Verstreute Tagebuchaufzeichnungen, December, 1911, in *Dichtungen und Schriften*, III, 175.

CHAPTER 4

1. See 10.31.1905, 11.16.1906, 1.3.1907, 3.4.1907, 10.14.1908, 12.13.1908, 12.20.1908.

CHAPTER 5

1. Walter Sokel, *The Writer in Extremis. Expressionism in 20th Century German Literature* (Stanford, 1959), p. 98.
2. Kasimir Edschmid, "Über den dichterischen Expressionismus," *Frühe Manifeste. Epochen des Expressionismus*. die mainzer reihe Dokumentar Veröffentlichungen (Hamburg, 1957), I, 34.
3. *Die Dramatischen Werke*, I, 712-13. In the following page references, this source is identified as "Schnitzler."
4. Schnitzler, p. 714.
5. *Ibid.*
6. *Ibid.*, p. 718.
7. *Ibid.*, p. 716.
8. Greulich, p. 145.

CHAPTER 6

1. "Die Menschen stehen vorwärts in den Strassen."
2. *Ophelia.*
3. *Lyrik des expressionistischen Jahrzehnts*, p. 110.

4. "Die Mühlen."

5. See Wolfgang Kayser, *Das Groteske in Malerei und Dichtung* (Hamburg, 1960), p. 130.

6. *Ibid.*, pp. 41 ff.

7. *Ibid.*, p. 137.

8. See H. Schelowsky, *Das Erlebnis der Groszstadt und seine Gestaltung in der neueren Lyrik* (Munich, Würzburg, 1937).

9. Soergel, *Neue Folge*, pp. 426-27.

10. F. J. Schneider, p. 146. See also Walter Muschg, *Von Trakl zu Brecht* (Munich, 1961), p. 29.

11. *Lyrik des expressionistischen Jahrzehnts*, p. 37.

12. *Menschheitsdämmerung*, p. 44.

13. *Ibid.*, p. 55.

14. *Ibid.*, p. 47.

15. Jean Paul Sartre, *Baudelaire* (Paris, 1947), p. 122.

16. Hugo Friedrich, *Die Struktur der modernen Lyrik* (Hamburg, 1956), p. 56.

17. *Ibid.*, p. 59.

18. *Ibid.*, p. 31.

19. *Ibid.*, p. 53.

20. "Berlin," *Menschheitsdämmerung*, p. 44.

21. "Verdammte Jugend," *Menschheitsdämmerung*, p. 54.

22. "Junger Prophet," *Lyrik des expressionistischen Jahrzehnts*, p. 117.

23. *Menschheitsdämmerung*, p. 84.

24. "Halber Schlaf."

25. Kayser, p. 136.

26. *Ibid.*, p. 137.

27. See Gen. 19:24.

28. Johannes Pfeiffer, "Georg Heym: *Der Krieg*," *Wege zum Gedicht*, ed. Rupert Hirschenauer and Albrecht Weber (Munich, 1956), pp. 349 ff.

29. Friedrich Leiner, "Georg Heym: *Der Krieg*," *Interpretationen moderner Lyrik* (Frankfurt/M, 1958), pp. 48 ff.

30. See Rainer Maria Rilke, "Die Aufzeichnungen des Malte Laurids Brigge," *Schriften in Prosa* (Leipzig, 1930), Part 2, pp. 13-14. Rilke also stresses that death in the modern world is mass produced, standardized, and anonymous.

31. Quoted from Charles C. Barber, *An Old High German Reader* (Oxford, 1951), pp. 80-81.

32. Other examples are "Die Stadt" and "Die Nacht III" (from *Der Himmel Trauerspiel*).

33. "Die Schläfer."

34. "Die Irren" (Variant).

35. "Die Nacht II" (from *Umbra Vitae*).

36. "Die Vögel."

37. "Helian," *Menschheitsdämmerung*, p. 110.

38. "Mondaufgang," *Menschheitsdämmerung*, p. 172.

39. "Ein Lied," *Menschheitsdämmerung*, p. 148.

40. "Gesang," *Menschheitsdämmerung*, p. 323.

41. "Gedichte," *Menschheitsdämmerung*, p. 317.

42. *Zarathustra*, Part 2, "Der Wahrsager," and "Von der unbefleckten Erkenntnis," respectively.

43. *Menschheitsdämmerung*, p. 312.

44. "Nebel," *Menschheitsdämmerung*, p. 59.

45. "Die Somnambulen."

46. "Die Vorstadt."
47. "Lichter gehen jetzt die Tage."
48. "Die Nacht III" (from *Der Himmel Trauerspiel*).
49. Mautz, pp. 256 ff.
50. *Dichtungen und Schriften*, II, 21.
51. "Die Heimat der Toten II."
52. "Ein Herbst-Abend."
53. "Die Nacht III" (from *Der Himmel Trauerspiel*).

CHAPTER 7

1. *Neues Tageblatt und General Anzeiger für Stuttgart und Württemberg* of January 14, 1911.
2. Sigmund Freud, "Die infantile Wiederkehr des Totemismus," *Totem und Tabu* (Hamburg, 1956), p. 174.
3. Seelig, p. 206.
4. Fritz Martini, *Das Wagnis der Sprache* (Stuttgart, 1954), pp. 260 ff.

CHAPTER 8

1. For this and the following paragraph, see my monograph *Style and Society in German Literary Expressionism*.
2. *Hörwerke der Zeit 2*, Hans Bredow-Institut (Hamburg, 1958).
3. Fritz Martini, "Georg Heym: *Der Krieg*," *Die deutsche Lyrik. Form und Geschichte*, ed. Benno von Wiese (Düsseldorf, 1956), II, 425 ff.
4. Wilhelm Emrich, *Franz Kafka* (Frankfurt/M, Bonn, 1961), p. 260.
5. Siegfried Lenz, "Zeit der Schuldigen," *Zeit der Schuldlosen. Zeit der Schuldigen* (Hamburg, 1961), p. 47.

Bibliography

EDITIONS OF WORKS BY GEORG HEYM, ARRANGED CHRONOLOGICALLY

Der Athener Ausfahrt. Trauerspiel in 1 Aufzug. Würzburg, 1907.
Der ewige Tag. Leipzig, 1911.
Umbra vitae. Nachgelassene Gedichte, ed. David Baumgardt, Golo Gangi (Erwin Loewenson), W. S. Ghuttmann, Jakob van Hoddis and Robert Jentzsch. Leipzig, 1912.
Der Dieb. Ein Novellenbuch. Leipzig, 1913.
Marathon, ed. Balduin von Möllhausen. Berlin-Wilmersdorf, 1914.
Dichtungen, ed. Kurt Pinthus and Erwin Loewenson. Munich, 1922.
Umbra vitae, with 47 original woodcuts by Ernst Ludwig Kirchner. Munich, 1924. (Facsimile ed. in Die Insel Bücherei, No. 749.)
Vier Gedichte, Papillons-Handdruck VI. Basel, 1946.
Gesammelte Gedichte. Mit einer Darstellung seines Lebens und Sterbens, ed. Carl Seelig. Zürich, 1947.
Marathon, ed. Karl Ludwig Schneider. Maximilian Gesellschaft, 1956.
Dichtungen und Schriften. Gesamtausgabe in vier Bänden, ed. Karl Ludwig Schneider: Vol. III, Tagebücher Träume Briefe, Hamburg, Munich, 1960; Vol. II, Prosa und Dramen, 1962; Vol. I, Lyrik, 1964.
Gedichte und Prosa, ed. Hans Rauschning. Hamburg, 1962.

COMPREHENSIVE BIBLIOGRAPHIES OF SECONDARY LITERATURE ON GEORG HEYM, ARRANGED CHRONOLOGICALLY

Heinrich Ellermann. "Georg Heym, Ernst Stadler, Georg Trakl. Drei Frühvollendete. Versuch einer geistesgeschichtlichen Bibliographie," Imprimatur. Ein Jahrbuch für Bücherfreunde, V. Hamburg, 1934.
Hans Bolliger. Bibliography in Georg Heym. Gesammelte Gedichte, ed. Carl Seelig. Zürich, 1947.
Kurt Mautz. Mythologie und Gesellschaft im Expressionismus. Die Dichtung Georg Heyms. Frankfurt/M, Bonn, 1961.

SELECTIVE LIST OF SECONDARY LITERATURE ON GEORG HEYM,
ARRANGED ALPHABETICALLY

Brand, Guido K. "Die Ahnung des Krieges. Georg Heym," *Die Frühvollendeten.* Berlin, Leipzig, 1929.

Erne, Nino. "Georg Heym," *Welt und Wort. Literarische Monatsschrift,* IV (1949), 312-15.

Eykman, Christoph. *Die Funktion des Hässlichen in der Lyrik Georg Heyms, Georg Trakls und Gottfried Benns.* Bonn, 1965.

Fritz, Walter Helmut. "Georg Heym," *Triffst du nur das Zauberwort,* ed. Jürgen Petersen, pp. 255-67. Frankfurt/M, 1961.

Greulich, Helmut. *Georg Heym, 1887-1912. Leben und Werk.* Berlin, 1931.

Grote, Christian. "Wortarten, Wortstellung und Satz im lyrischen Werk Georg Heyms." Unpublished dissertation, University of Munich, 1962.

Hirschenauer, Rupert. "Georg Heym. *Tod des Pierrots,*" *Interpretationen moderner Lyrik,* pp. 48-59. Frankfurt/M, Berlin, Bonn, 1957.

Kohlschmidt, Werner. "Der deutsche Frühexpressionismus im Werke Georg Heyms und Georg Trakls," *Orbis Litterarum,* IX, 1 (1954), 3-17.

Krispyn, Egbert. "Sources and Subject Matter in Two Short Stories by Georg Heym," *AUMLA. Journal of the Australasian Universities Language and Literature Association,* 12 (November, 1959), 52-57.

———. "Georg Heyms Prosasammlung *Der Dieb*—ein Novellenbuch?" *Levende Talen,* 215 (June, 1962), 352-62.

———. "Georg Heym und der Neue Club," *Revista de Letras* (Assis), IV (1963), 262-71.

Lange, Horst. "Georg Heym. Bildnis eines Dichters," *Akzente. Zeitschrift für Dichtung,* I, 2 (1954), 180-87.

Loewenson, Erwin. *Georg Heym oder Vom Geist des Schicksals.* Hamburg, Munich, 1962.

Mahlendorf, Ursula R. "Georg Heym. Stil und Weltbild." Unpublished dissertation, Brown University, 1958 (*Dissertation Abstracts,* XIX, 3, 1759).

———. "The Myth of Evil. The Reevaluation of the Judaic-Christian Tradition in the Work of Georg Heym," *The Germanic Review,* XXXVI (1961), 180-94.

———. "Georg Heym's Development as a Dramatist and Poet," *JEGP,* LXIII, 1 (1964), 58-71.

Martens, Gunter. "*Umbra Vitae* und *Der Himmel Trauerspiel.* Die ersten Sammlungen der nachgelassenen Gedichte Georg Heyms," *Euphorion,* LIX, 1/2 (1965).

Martini, Fritz. "Georg Heym. *Der Krieg,*" *Die deutsche Lyrik. Form und Geschichte. Interpretationen,* ed Benno von Wiese, II, 425-49. Düsseldorf, 1956.

———. "Georg Heym. *Die Sektion,*" *Das Wagnis der Sprache,* pp. 260 ff. Stuttgart, 1954.

Mautz, Kurt. *Mythologie und Gesellschaft im Expressionismus. Die Dichtung Georg Heyms.* Frankfurt/M, Bonn, 1961.

Milch, Werner. "Georg Heym," *Schlesische Monatshefte,* VIII (1931), 520-24.

Motekat, Helmut. "Georg Heym. *Umbra vitae.* Interpretationen," *Deutschunterricht für Ausländer,* VII (1957), 65-72.

Pfeiffer, Johannes. "Über Georg Heyms Gedicht *Der Krieg,*" *Wege zum Gedicht,* ed. Rupert Hirschenauer and Albrecht Weber, pp. 349 ff. Munich, 1956. Also in Pfeiffer. *Über das Dichterische und den Dichter. Beiträge zum Verständnis deutscher Dichtung,* pp. 118-21. Hamburg, 1956.

Schneider, Ferdinand Josef. *Der expressive Mensch und die deutsche Lyrik der Gegenwart.* Stuttgart, 1927.

Schneider, Karl Ludwig, *Der bildhafte Ausdruck in den Dichtungen Georg Heyms, Georg Trakls und Ernst Stadlers.* Heidelberg, 1954.

Schulz, Eberhard August Wilhelm. "Das Problem des Menschen bei Georg Heym." Unpublished dissertation, Kiel, 1953.

Schwarz, Georg. *Georg Heym. Genius der Deutschen.* Mühlacker, 1963. The title and reputable publisher—Stieglitz Verlag—are misleading. This work is a worthless compilation of distorted facts and wrong judgments, based on falsified documents.

Stadler, Ernst. "Georg Heym: *Der ewige Tag,*" *Cahiers Alsaciens,* I, 3 (1912), 144-46. Also in *Dichtungen,* ed. Karl Ludwig Schneider, II, 11-13. Hamburg, n.d.

Uhlig, Helmut. "Visionär des Chaos. Ein Versuch über Georg Heym," *Der Monat. Internationale Zeitschrift für Politik und geistiges Leben,* VI, 64 (1954), 417-27.

————. "Vom Ästhetizismus zum Expressionismus. Ernst Stadler, Georg Heym und Georg Trakl," *Expressionismus. Gestalten einer literarischen Bewegung,* ed. Hermann Friedmann and Otto Mann. Heidelberg, 1956.